STEEL 2050

How Steel Transformed the World and Now Must Transform Itself

by
Rod Beddows

Devonian Ventures

Kingsbridge, Devon, UK

Copyright © 2014 by **Rod Beddows**

All rights reserved. No part of this publication may be reproduced, distributed or transmitted in any form or by any means, without prior written permission.

Devonian Ventures
Leigh Barton House
Kingsbridge, Devon, TQ7 4AG
United Kingdom

rbeddows@hcfintl.com

Although every precaution has been taken in the preparation of this book, the publisher and author assume no responsibility for errors or omissions. Neither is any liability assumed for damages resulting from the use of this information contained herein.

Steel 2050 / Rod Beddows. -- 1st ed.
ISBN 978-0-9930381-0-5

CONTENTS

Steel has transformed the world 1
Steel and its discontents 19
The reality of the diagnosis 29
Forecasting and its discontents 47
Long run drivers of steel demand 67
Is there growth after China? 95
The growth model for the next 20 113
Funding the growth 127
Solving the funding crisis: Delivering service 143
Finding contentment: Managing volatility 159
Technology 179
An industry for the 21st century 191

LIST OF EXHIBITS

1.1: Total accumulated global steel production	6
1.2: UK steel industry labour productivity	10
1.3: German steel industry rolled steel yield from crude steel	11
1.4: German steel industry energy efficiency and Co2 emissions	11
1.5: Global annual steel production	13
2.1: Historic steel industry ROCE and EBIT margin	20
2.2: Historic steel industry cash flows and EBITDA	21
2.3: EBITDA requirements for the steel industry	22
2.4: Global scenario challenges	27
3.1: Steel, scrap, and iron ore prices	38
3.2: Real annual iron ore prices 1968-2012	39
4.1: Marianne leading the sans culottes over the barricades	48
5.1: US steel consumption with net imports	69
5.2: Regional steel use by sector	74
5.3: Crude steel consumption growth trajectory	77
5.4: Apparent and true finished steel consumption per capita	81
5.5: World population, GDP, and steel consumption	87
5.6: Log base 2 global accumulated annual steel production	88
5.7: Steel consumption per capita forecast	91
5.8: World mine production and reserves	93
6.1: The 20/20 countries and their steel use	101
7.1: Global trade as a fraction of global GDP	122
8.1: What returns can a greenfield steel plant expect?	136
9.1: Car with 3 wheels	148

9.2: Performance record for an actual steel mill	150
10.1: Iron ore futures and derivatives trading volumes	162
10.2: ArcelorMittal Europe price list	168
10.3: Cost of capital for different industries	173
10.4: Weekly indexed price for Nickel, HRC and Oil	176
12.1: Steel industry scorecard	194

FOREWORD

It is a pleasure for me to write this foreword for Rod's important book.

Our industry faces many challenges, but this is not new. It also has in prospect many exciting opportunities; the world needs steel to build a better future for our 6.5 billion people. Here in India we know that as much as anyone. It is exciting and fulfilling to embrace these prospects and meet these challenges.

I have known Rod Beddows for many years. I have always found his views perceptive, his willingness to engage with executives stimulating and his creative contributions most valuable. I know many others in our industry who agree with me. His long experience of the industry and his independence give him a unique position from which to offer us his wisdom.

Perhaps now, more than ever, we need innovation in the ways we do business. The world around us is changing technologically, geo-politically and in terms of human aspirations. We need to change with it. Rod raises many important issues and problems; he also challenges many accepted opinions and views. Wherever he challenges he also provides proposals for solutions. He engages with the urgency of our needs within the context of a long term perspective which is unusual but very necessary.

Most of all his book is a most enjoyable and stimulating read. I hope you enjoy it.

Sajjan Jindal, Chairman and Managing Director, JSW Steel

PREFACE

> *"When I was young, I found out that the big toe always ends up making a hole in the sock. So I gave up wearing socks."* Albert Einstein

Why should I write this book? Who should read it?

I have spent the greatest portion of my professional life working in the ferrous sector as an adviser in strategy and corporate finance. The industry is fascinating in its history, complexity and the plethora of characters who inhabit it. Every type of character is here and every nationality. The ferrous sector is essentially "steel": 99% of iron ore goes to steelmaking, the overwhelming proportion of alloying elements such as chrome, nickel and manganese also go into steelmaking. Even 50% of zinc goes into coating flat rolled steel and steel components. I shall, therefore, use the term "ferrous" interchangeably with steel.

What actually started me on writing this book was a consideration of the position of a young person, say 25 years old, who is just entering into a career in the steel industry. Maybe this young person is from a developing country such as India where the sector is vibrant and fundamental to the whole country's future. What would I want to say to them so that they could learn from my experience and failures?

This does not mean that only 25 year old Indians should read this book! In fact, I want to encourage youthful talent to see the ferrous sector as exciting and full of potential. Today, young intelligent people see the electronics, software and related worlds as the future and tend to seek entry to those spheres. This was different in the 19th and early 20th centuries when metals production and application was the industrial frontier that telecommunications and information technology are today. Perhaps I can encourage talented youth to see the industry differently because the future health of any activity is dependent on the talent it can attract to meet its challenges.

I hope other audiences will also enjoy this work as we all use and benefit from steel products. Those in the various activities and institutions of banking, known as "the City", will benefit from understanding what to look for in the companies likely to perform better financially than others. Likewise, we nearly all have pensions, a proportion of which is invested in shares of mining and steel companies. As I will show, the financial sector has a major contribution to make to the industry's future success.

Those who are at all interested in the economic development of the world in the past, in the present and in the future, cannot escape the importance of steel and steelmaking raw materials to that development.

Finally, I wanted to write the book that I would have wanted to read when I first became involved in the industry 40 years ago.

This book, therefore, is a distillation of my learning, experiences, failures and successes. Somewhat informally and as a frame of reference for thinking, it takes three timescales: five, 15 and 50 years into the future. These are appropriate in different ways. If I was 25 years old again I would be interested in what my industry might look like in 50 years' time when I will have reached the end of my career; for we will all retire at later ages in the future. This perspective would be critically important in orienting what I think and do and what I might wish to change. It happens that 50 years is also the planning horizon for a major iron ore mine.

In a heavy industry of steel's complexity, with large amounts of capital to be deployed in any capital program, 15 years is the appropriate planning horizon for a new steelmaking or processing asset. For operational and budgeting planning, then five years is appropriate. Business cycles are particularly acute in upstream industries such as commodities and steel and these are normally shorter than five years, so that period should capture the vicissitudes of the cycle.

This book is not a text book. It does not seek to be academic and has few references. It is not scientific – it does not seek to prove anything. It is not comprehensive in history or topic. It is certainly not technical – the industry places far too much faith in operational and technical achievement. Instead, it seeks to be polemical and challenging, and also truly strategic in the sense of encouraging creative thought and reflection about the long-term opportunities and challenges. Perhaps, in time, this strategic thinking might lead to the formulation of fresh initiatives based on new insights which, when adopted, might lead to improved economic performance and enhanced success for the 25-year-olds entering the industry.

This is an adventure story, for industrial development is an adventure into unknown waters of innovation, change and opportunity. It is an essay rather than a thesis. The writer asks only that the reader has an open mind. Much that is taken for granted in the ferrous sector is a sacred cow, formed of long-repeated behaviour and consensual thinking. Institutions, like individuals, find it difficult to learn. When we see something not working well, our first and often only instinct is to repeat what did not work--but faster, harder and more expensively, with the same failures as a result. To change a response is seen as painful. The pain and discomfort of the formulation and adoption of new responses to failure - to learn - is difficult. The discomfort is also immediate and avoidance of such is a natural but destructive human habit.

Over my life, I have formed the conclusion that economic challenges are simple of solution. The difficulties lie in institutional inertia. I formed this hypothesis very early on and hoped that experience would prove it false. Unfortunately, this hope was misplaced. I remain convinced that all problems in economics are easy to solve, but economists overcomplicate them. These complications justify more funding and importance for economists, and of course no social group can avoid the temptation to promote its own economic interests. In macroeconomics, politicians encourage this as it supports their institutional interest in finding "problems" requiring their action.

In any heavy industry we are dominated by large organisations with long institutional memories. These cannot avoid being barriers to rapid change. Institutional inertia is everywhere. To borrow from Jean-Jacques Rousseau, organisations are born free but are everywhere in chains. These chains are largely self-imposed, as we will see. The least painful source of change is leadership within the industry, self-generated or brought in as in the case of the growth of Mittal Steel or Nucor, the two most innovative steel groups of the last generation.

The only alternative mode of change is extinction and replacement by other industries and structures. This can happen as when the horse-drawn carriage industry was replaced by the automobile industry or typewriters by word processors. In the case of steel, this cannot happen as the product is fundamental to civilised life. It is essential that the industry change for the benefit of all of us. Perhaps a book such as this will encourage new thinking, and new managers and leaders to use those ideas to improve economic performance.

The people who I hope will read this book are numerous. There are about 10 million people employed directly in the ferrous sector and many more dependent on it and its products. I would hope anyone within the industry in an executive position, or aspiring to fill such a position, would find something of value. In addition, much of the book discusses various aspects of the steel market and how customers can be better served. The number of organisations using steel products is in the tens of millions and each of these organisations can, I hope, find something of interest here.

Finally, there are all the observers and analysts including financial analysts, economists, consultants and others with a general interest in the industry and industrial development in general.

As with any book, I hope to entertain and engage the reader in a pleasurable experience which will be worthwhile and – most importantly - not too long. My ambition as a writer is best described by William Cowper:

A tale should be judicious, clear, succinct;
The language plain, and incidents well linked;
Tell not as new what ev'rybody knows,
And new or old, still hasten to a close.

ACKNOWLEDGEMENTS

Over a career of many years there are too many people who have, either contributed to my thinking, or on whose thinking I have built. Many colleagues and clients could be mentioned but if I attempted a long list I would surely miss some and would not like to offend.

More recently, as part of the actual production of this book, a number of people have helped substantially whom I would like to mention. Most especially is Mike Walsh, always positive and willing to be both critical and supportive at the right points. In the production of the exhibits and general conversations, in addition to Mike, I would like to thank David Tucker, Vijay Thangavelu and Alex Gurkov. More generally, I owe much to colleagues at Hatch and HCF, and to Hatch for their permission to access data in their files.

In editing and improving the script again my thanks go to Mike and to Mark Bell and Cathy Randall. In the task of getting the finished article into readable format and out into the wide world I will thank Caroline Macmillan.

Thanks also go to "the princess" and to Holly for their help in ways that only they know.

PROLOGUE

This book can be summarised as trying to answer the problem posed by the first quotation within the context of the second. These two statements encapsulate my entire purpose and serve as a succinct prologue.

> *"Innovation, probably here is the biggest challenge for all of us: how to think out of the box? How to reinvent ourselves? One thing is for sure. The way it's going it's going to take longer. We don't see that many changes. We have got to act. We cannot continue to do the same thing we have been doing. I mean the results are right in front of us"*
>
> Andre Gerdau Johannpeter. CEO. Gerdau. *Extract from speech at the Steel Success Strategies XXVIII. New York. June 2013*

> *"It is common to hear people say how much the epoch of enormous economic progress .... Is over; that the rapid improvement in the standard of life is now going to slow down....; that a decline in prosperity is more likely than an improvement....*
>
> *I believe that this is a wildly mistaken interpretation of what is happening to us. We are suffering....from the growing-pains of over-rapid changes, from the painfulness of readjustment between one economic period and another...*
>
> *Mankind is solving its economic problem. I would predict that the standard of life in progressive countries one hundred years hence will be between four and eight times as high as it is today"*
>
> J. M. Keynes, 1930. From; *"Economic possibilities for our grandchildren". The Nation and Athenaeum. January 11th and 18th 1930.*

CHAPTER ONE

Steel has transformed the world

"The only end of writing is to enable the readers better to enjoy life, or better to endure it" Samuel Johnson

Steel has been a fascination, a subject of study, and a profession for me for over 40 years. It is not an exaggeration to say that the problems of the ferrous world have been a matter of a long intellectual love affair. My first experience was as a junior consultant working with a Scandinavian consulting firm for Uddeholm Bruks after the first oil price crisis in 1974. The crisis had shattered the markets and expectations for the company--and it was in dire trouble. The remnants of Uddeholm are now parts of Bohler and Outokumpu.

The industry's fascination for me takes many forms: partly it is the history, partly that it is fundamental to all industry - and indeed civilisation itself - yet it is perennially beset by economic problems and crises, being unable to find a long-term economic structure which is self-sustaining. This makes it the most anomalous of industries. As Churchill said of Russia, "It is a riddle, wrapped in a mystery inside an enigma." In short, it is a conundrum and this will be the underlying theme of this book.

As I sit here, beginning this book in the summer of 2012, in the drawing room of my house in Argyll, it seems a long way from the steel and ferrous industries and their concerns of financial viability. The environment is as close to being natural and unpolluted as is possible in Europe. It is under the almost permanent influence of winds coming off the Atlantic. There is no industry within sight, although wind turbines will shortly protrude from the top of the hills opposite. My ground contains over 1,500 varieties of trees and shrubs, a wide variety of animal life both aquatic and mammalian: red deer, roe deer, badgers, foxes, red squirrels; all are in abundance, as are over 120 species of birds. The arboretum behind the house contains many specimen trees, including exotic conifers from North America, Chile, China and what was once the British Empire. These do not constitute the native climax vegetation and without care and attention would eventually die out.

The native trees are oaks and birches intermixed with hawthorn, hazel and willow. In this woodland the oaks predominate. The whole of Argyll, up to approximately 300 feet above sea level, was covered by this native woodland until man's arrival in numbers. Humans cut this woodland to use as firewood but also to burn into charcoal to smelt iron. The iron resources were local small deposits of ironstone. The iron was transported to the nearby Clyde, originally to be used as iron, and later to be hammer-wrought into steel. In the 18th century this activity, plus the innate entrepreneurial creativity of the people, formed the basis for the emergence of Glasgow as the heavy- engineering capital of the world for a glorious 19th century of success. Adam Smith was Professor of Moral Philosophy at Glasgow University. Opposite my property is a small village called Furnace to where the local Campbell chieftains imported Lancashire ironmasters to found a large-scale, for then, blast furnace based iron industry in the 1750s. As a result of this industry, there are now only remnants of the original oak woods which we are now seeking to preserve.

The remains of iron-making in this area are also present from an earlier time. Up the hillside behind my house there is moorland and extensive plantations of commercial woodland. Here in the woods, and now very difficult to find, are the remains of 13th and 14th century bloomeries. These were primitive small-scale blast furnaces which are the earliest known relics of iron-making in the area.

The importance of metal

Iron, and its main alloy in the form of steel, have been a key to the last 4 millennia of human development and the discovery of how to make metal was a key innovation in human history. There have been three fundamental technological shifts in the history of man's economic and social development.

The first was the agrarian transformation started about 10,000 years ago in Mesopotamia and the Yangtze delta. This enabled humans to cultivate plants for food, thus releasing man from dependence on hunting and gathering. Agriculture enabled populations to grow and live in permanent settlements.

The second technological shift was the smelting and refining of metal, of which by far the most important was the making of iron followed later by steel. This ferrous material provides the means for the making of all tools, machines and equipment which enhances the effectiveness of human labour thus radically increasing the opportunities for leisure and creative endeavour. No other industrial innovation is so central to all others or has the same significance.

The third revolution is only in its early stages – that is the digitalisation of information and its mechanised processing at lightning speed. This revolution will transform the world again in ways that currently we can only see as through a fog; or as the Bible says "as through a glass darkly".

Iron is derived from iron oxide ore which has been smelted at high temperature with carbon to remove the oxygen and to leave relatively impure iron. If smelted with limestone, a slag removes the deleterious materials such as silica and alumina, producing a nearly pure and usable iron. With this, the Iron Age was born. As iron was the strongest metal then available, it displaced bronze. Those that could make it could have the best weapons and dominate in warfare and thus promote their forms of social organisation and their ideas. Very small quantities were made by today's standards: kilograms rather than millions of tonnes.

Not only did weapons improve and give political dominance to their owners, tools could be made which allowed the creation of products of great strength and utility, while employing less labour. Thus civilisation became possible. Without iron, agriculture was extremely inefficient and of low productivity. Only with agriculture employing relatively sophisticated iron-based tools such as ploughs and the equipment to tether oxen and horses to those ploughs, could food become substantially more plentiful; and then settled life in village communities and eventually cities could thrive. With more labour released from agriculture, other human activity could expand rapidly, allowing for new economic activity, new industries, complex culture and new forms of behaviour to evolve.

The primacy of steel

Iron is a poor material compared to steel. Making steel requires smelted iron to be refined with the addition of small quantities of alloying elements such as vanadium, boron, manganese, et al., which impart valuable and diverse properties to the iron increasing its utility in a wide variety of ways. Steel is, thus, an alloy not an element. Iron (Fe) is the main element in steel. Alloyed steel comes in thousands of different metallurgical variations, many more than with any other metal, all designed, or sometimes discovered by chance, to give different properties of ductility, strength and corrosion resistance, among other things.

Serendipity has often been important in the development of steel. Stainless steel was discovered by chance in Sheffield; although Krupp, the German company, would dispute this, claiming an almost simultaneous discovery although the grades and alloying elements were different. In 1913 Harry Brearley, a metallurgist, was testing all sorts of new alloys on a random basis to see what would happen in terms of ductility and other mechanical properties. He was not looking for corrosion resistance but rather heat resistance. The steels which he rejected as having no interesting properties he cast aside into a scrap pile for later re-melting and re-using. Looking at the pile one day he noticed that one of the pieces of metal had not rusted – so was stainless steel discovered.

These differences in properties are of critical importance and the infinite variety can lead to some important challenges as we shall see. The variety of products and qualities has enabled widespread innovation in all aspects of industry and commerce. However, the making of steel was hampered for thousands of years by the absence of a process which could make steel in sufficient quantity and reliable quality for general use, at acceptable cost. The breakthroughs came with Huntsman and later Bessemer. The latter's invention of his converter reduced the cost for conversion of iron to steel to a seventh of its previous level. Huntsman - as a clock, lock and tool maker - was a steel user, not producer, based in Sheffield. As with many other technological and industrial breakthroughs in so many industries, outsiders are the most effective originators of innovations. This is a lesson of great importance for the steel industry today. The most recent example of this is Nucor in the USA, which entered steel production also as a result of being a dissatisfied customer.

This wide variety of characteristics produced by alloying - and iron is compatible with many other elements - combined with cheapness, has guaranteed that steel predominates in total metal usage. Steel is only a third the cost of the next most commonly used metal, aluminium, and its market is 50 times as large.

The spread of steel production

The development of steel usage has been a remarkable phenomenon, facilitated by continuous innovation and increases in efficiency. The story is one which is very exciting to anyone interested in economics and human development. The annual world production of steel was less than 1 million tonnes when Bessemer's converter (for converting iron to steel) was introduced in the 1860s. The industry was overwhelmingly located in the UK and "Sheffield Steel" was a brand synonymous with quality, consistency and low cost.

A Krupp family member came to the UK, from Germany, to learn the secrets of production from the Sheffield Steel producers. The openness and misplaced confidence of the steel masters of Sheffield meant that he did not need to spy on them. Their secrets were easily obtained as they invited him to visit their factories and openly explained their techniques. He took his learning back to Germany and founded the modern German industry. It is thus that the late 19th century is a good starting point for considering the industry's growth and modern shape. By then Germany and the USA, where production technologies had also come from the UK and where demand had been boosted by the Civil War, had industries which were challenging the UK. The industry had become truly international.

EXHIBIT 1.1: TOTAL ACCUMULATED GLOBAL STEEL PRODUCTION/Mt

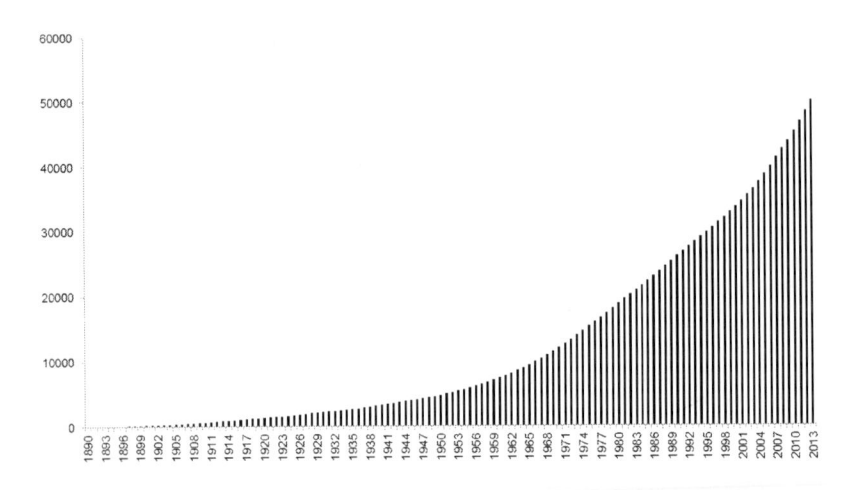

Source: worldsteel, Zimmerman and Hatch

Over the last 125 years a total of 50 billion tonnes of steel have been made. The total number is growing at over 1.5 bn tp.a. or approximately 3%, and the rate of growth has recently accelerated due to Chinese production. As we will see, the world is likely to require about 4 bn tp.a. by the middle of this century. Steel shows no sign of declining in utility and requirement. In fact, the age of steel is only in its infancy. The future is at least as exciting as the past.

Steel has transformed the world

Without steel all aspects of life would be more difficult, more expensive or impossible. Many are the unforeseen but desirable consequences from steel's use. The steel bicycle led to the demise of the village idiot for the simple reason that young men and women could now seek partners from outside their inbred village communities. Cheap transport plus packaging and refrigeration, all dependent on steel material for their construction, has led to a doubling in the efficiency of agricultural production in industrialised nations as they have enabled more food to reach consumers in an edible condition. The introduction of such modern methods in developing countries such as India will make a very large, and underestimated, contribution to solving any perceived food shortage. In India less than 50% of farm production reaches the consumer compared to over 90% in the USA. This depends on steel.

The building and construction industries have been revolutionised by the use of steel to enable high rise buildings and the industrialisation, by prefabrication, of much construction. In the home, domestic drudgery has been replaced by appliances. All the factories and processing plants which manufacture the components and finished products facilitating our modern life require steel in the form of machine tools, machinery in general and processing plants. The electricity we depend on for all this convenience is made cheaply by steel turbines and boilers and distributed by steel reinforced wires supported by steel gantries.

But steel does not just make life more convenient and efficient; it can lead to the transformation of social structure itself. We are all somewhat familiar with the industrial revolution and the mechanisation of production processes. These changes required urbanisation and large work forces, highly organised and better educated, which themselves underpinned the emergence of mass democracy. Another social upheaval was a consequence of a very small steel product (actually wrought iron, but that is an early related form of steel) innovation – the stirrup.

Iron and steel have always been important in the development of weapons but the story of the stirrup is one of a very small innovation leading to a major structural impact in all aspects of society. Before this invention, armies were essentially infantry. Cavalry existed as a scouting force and for the rapid movement of troops which, when fighting, often dismounted and became infantry. If they fought on horseback then they used only the same weapons as the infantry. Cavalry were mounted infantry because they had no means of tightly controlling the horse at high speed and of securing their position in the saddle – if they had one at all – if they were carrying heavy weapons.

The stirrup changed all this. It enabled the mounted man to be secure and to control the horse effectively. By having a secure position in the saddle the weight of equipment could be increased, so the use of heavy lances and swords developed, and heavy armour could be worn, providing protection. Perhaps, most importantly, the rider could charge without fear of falling off or losing control of his mount. The charging, armour-protected and heavily-armed knight became the mediaeval equivalent of the 20th century tank.

The dominance of the mounted knight is, for the English, most clearly shown by the Normans. Not only did they conquer England but this small tribe of displaced Norse also controlled Normandy and Sicily for a period of over 100 years. They were the mounted knight par excellence. The social and economic consequences were dramatic. The economic activity that was required to support a knight was new and transformational. He required armour and heavy fighting equipment, so metal working and blacksmithing were required more than ever before. He needed a large number of horses for not only did he need one for the battle, and often replacements for that, but also horses to transport his equipment. These horses required agricultural production and space. One horse requires four acres of pasture and also land for hay and fodder production for winter. A horse requires tending all the time, and much labour has to be devoted to this task.

The organisation of social life was changed beyond recognition from the Saxon period. The medieval manorial village arose where the free peasants of Saxon times - free legally and free to move and relocate and change occupation - became un-free serfs, close to being slaves without the chance of movement in occupation or place of abode. Their freedom had to be curtailed to enable knights to be provided for on a reliable basis. Infantry could carry their equipment with them and needed little in comparison to an armoured knight. The manorial village was the social form whereby the lord of the manor, a knight or a nobleman obligated to provide one or more knights for the king, was supported. The social fabric of England and Western Europe as a whole was transformed – and all precipitated by the simple stirrup.

Steel is massively more efficient

The volume of steel production today is supported by, and partly caused by, the vast improvements in efficiency of production. At the labour intensity of 50 years ago, it would take 150 million people to manufacture today's annual steel production. If the productivity of the best steel plants of today were replicated worldwide, a labour force of no more than 10 million would be required although additional labour would be necessary to mine the raw materials and transport the material to steel plants and then on to end customers. The industry is ten times more labour-efficient now, than 50 years ago.

EXHIBIT 1.2: UK STEEL INDUSTRY LABOUR PRODUCTIVITY (t crude steel/employee)

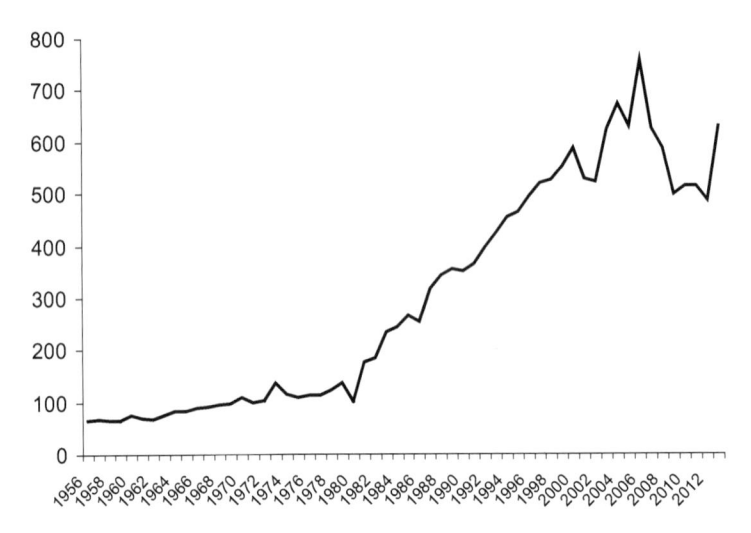

Source: UK Steel, worldsteel and Hatch

Likewise, efficiency improvements in process yield and energy utilisation have followed labour efficiency. The application of process control and automation, process integration and the elimination of entire process stages, such as the use of continuous casting, have improved through yield; that is the yield through the full manufacturing process from raw materials to finished steel products, by 40% in 40 years, so that less crude steel is required for a fixed quantity of finished product. Significant reductions in energy use and in carbon and other emissions have been achieved as a result

In addition, steel is infinitely recyclable. The only limitation on total recycling is that certain applications result in some steel being effectively "lost" due to being used down holes in the ground or under water and other inaccessible places and a small percentage erodes as rust. When recycled , by virtue of the electric arc furnace (EAF), it is also produced using much less energy than through the blast furnace (BF) route because the process starts with steel which only needs remelting and not, as with the BF, smelting from virgin iron ore. Eventually 80%, or perhaps more, of all steel production will be via the scrap recycled route using the EAF. Improvements in the EAF route have led to the explosion of scrap recycling over the last 50 years.

EXHIBIT 1.3: GERMAN STEEL INDUSTRY ROLLED STEEL YIELD FROM CRUDE STEEL/%

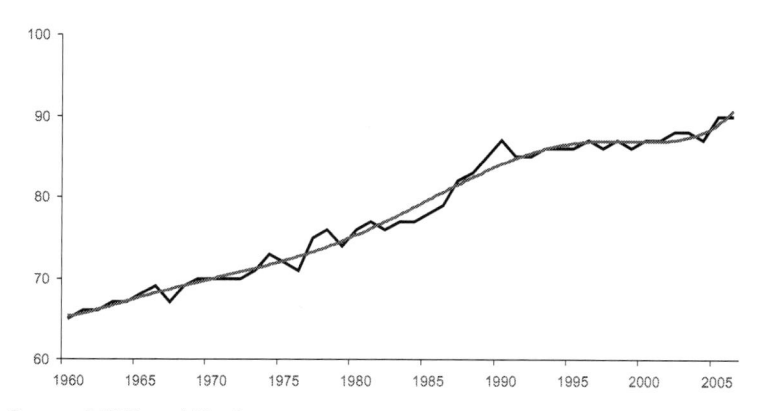

Source: VDEh and Hatch

EXHIBIT 1.4: GERMAN STEEL INDUSTRY ENERGY EFFICIENCY (GJ/t Crude Steel) AND CO2 EMISSIONS (CO2 t /t Crude Steel)

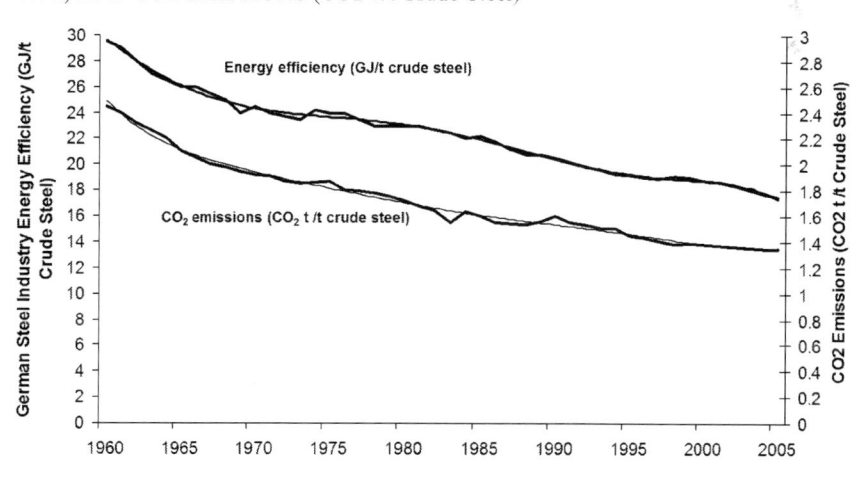

Source: VDEh and Hatch

The price of basic grades of steel today is about $800 /t. The higher grades for demanding applications such as body panels for cars are $1,500 /t. There is a small percentage of production, less than 3%, which is much more expensive (e.g. tool, stainless and electrical steels), but as a general rule an average of $1,000 /t is a good estimate for the price of steel today. The price varies greatly over the economic and industry cycle: over the last 10 years by as much as 100%, trough to peak. We will examine the consequences and challenges of this variation in detail later. This price should be put into perspective – in an average automobile there is no more than 1.5 t of steel, at ex-mill weight, so about $2,250 worth at the most. This is only one and a half week's earnings for the average employed person in the USA. Today, the cost of transforming raw materials into steel in North America is the same as in 1865 at the end of the Civil War – that is in nominal dollar terms. In other words, the industry has managed to absorb all the inflation in energy, labour and other costs, excluding raw materials. Effectively, all the increase in costs which are within the producers' control or influence has been absorbed, over the last 150 years.

Supported by these improvements and the continuous innovation in grades and varieties of steel alloy, there is no sign of a slowdown in steel demand growth. Indeed, the speed of growth has accelerated and over our period of 120 years has easily exceeded the growth of world GDP at 4.0% p.a. against approximately 3.4% p.a. for GDP.

Steel is ubiquitous both in its use in our lives and in its impact through history, due to the twin characteristics of its cheapness and its range of attributes. Wherever you are sitting and reading this you will be surrounded by steel in a myriad of uses. Your Kindle will have a little steel in it somewhere, as will your laptop or desk. Your office building, the machinery in your factory and the train or car which took you there this morning – all will require substantial quantities of steel by weight. No part of our civilisation could be supported without steel. By value, it is the second largest commodity industry after oil and gas, and represents approximately 3 - 4% of global GDP when all its forms and varieties are accounted for.

EXHIBIT 1.5: GLOBAL ANNUAL STEEL PRODUCTION/Mt

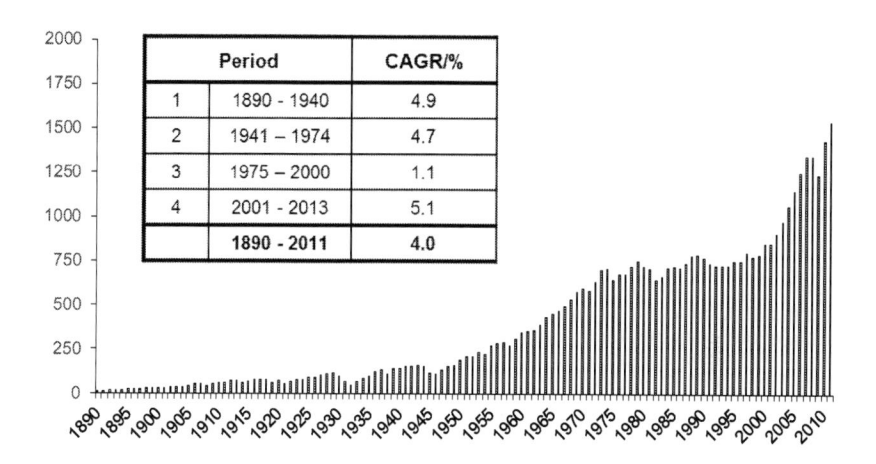

	Period	CAGR/%
1	1890 - 1940	4.9
2	1941 – 1974	4.7
3	1975 – 2000	1.1
4	2001 - 2013	5.1
	1890 - 2011	4.0

Source: worldsteel, Zimmerman and Hatch

Against this backdrop of improvements in qualities, growth of demand, improvements in efficiency, environmental friendliness, and with a market and demand that grows faster than world GDP, it would be normal to expect a strong financial performance and an industry in good health. Yet the steel industry regularly experiences periods of crisis and poor economic performance. Indeed poor performance for shareholders is the norm. Perhaps 8 years out of 10, the industry fails to meet its cost of capital. In mid-2013 the deputy chairman of Tata Steel Group, voiced his view that the total industry worldwide would register a financial loss in 2013. In addition the chairman of what was Nippon Steel in early 2012 opined that the world had reached "peak steel", that demand had peaked for the future and the industry was facing a future of no demand growth.

Steel's financial performance is poor

Currently the industry is in a severe downturn and beset by problems which are repetitive and endemic. Reading the statements of company chairmen and industry leaders seems depressingly redolent of previous decades: complaints of overcapacity, volatility in price, volatility in demand, "excessive" raw material prices, fragmentation of structure, political interference and state subsidy proliferate. These complaints and problems existed in the 1930s, 1970s, 1980s and repeat themselves today: it would seem urgent that something new must be done.

The industry has not been idle in the face of this repetitive issue. Any industry requires an underlying economic equation which allows for the generation of returns on capital which encourage reinvestment and new investment for growth. The equation is set by the margin generated by revenues less costs over the quantum of capital employed to generate the revenue. Management works on the various elements; margin can be improved by reducing costs or improving selling prices or both. Fixed capital can be reduced by asset optimisation, rationalisation, or new technology; whilst working capital can be reduced by simplified supply chains or different terms of payment along the chain.

Management actions have led to the huge gains in productivity and efficiency observed earlier. This process is continuous and on-going. It becomes intensified when demand slumps as happened recently; whilst in periods of growth, attention is concentrated on exploiting this growth to widen margins and improve returns on capital whilst maintaining, or even enhancing, market position.

However, experience shows that the gains in cost reduction are perpetually "given away" to customers and replicated by competitors. The replication is encouraged and facilitated by the intensely collaborative nature of steel producers. All major members of the industry and most minor members belong to a global fraternity, institutionalised as the World Steel Association (worldsteel). Amongst other activities this has numerous working groups focused on improvements to be shared amongst all members. A truly noble and socially useful purpose – but hardly likely to result in improved financial, rather than economic, performance; the former requires either competitive differentiation or improvements in the way customers are serviced. Costs are reduced and new products developed but shared across the industry: thus gains are replicated. This would be attractive if gains were not given away to customers – but that is what happens. This is of the greatest importance and I will address the challenge of how to avoid this, and thus how the industry can retain some if not all of its gains in efficiency, in a later chapter.

In my experience of working across various industries I have never come across one which shares so many ideas, norms of behaviour, training and educational background, and social working groups as the steel industry. It is an industry which has a very strong sense of its own identity which breeds strong camaraderie, but also breeds homogeneity which is detrimental to improved financial performance for this requires innovation and innovation in turn requires divergent views, opinions and experiences to provide the "gene pool" for the generation of innovative "mutations".

Historical focus on margin enhancement has also been on improving selling price and through product innovation. The advances in cold rolling, galvanising, then other forms of coating plus the continuous development of new grades, is very impressive. Now grades of high strength and so called advanced high strength steels are in increasing use. Such grades lead to lighter gauges being required and so less steel by weight. This enhances such efficiencies as energy use in vehicles. However, nothing in history suggests that the economic benefits will flow through to the steel producer for anything other than a short time. Here the key lies in the world of customer service. An innovative product alone is insufficient to produce an improved return.

More recently two other lines of attack have been used to improve performance: backward integration and consolidation. The privatised steel groups which came out of the collapsed Soviet empire, and also those groups that benefitted by the acquisition of ex-communist assets, such as Mittal Steel, realised and demonstrated the virtues of backward integration, especially into iron ore mines. Across the business cycle, owning these operating assets resulted in wider operating margins and more resilience to finished steel product price declines in downturns. This experience has been reinforced by the results of certain Indian and Brazilian groups. Perhaps as much as 30% of global steel production benefits from this backward integration. As an interesting historical comment, all steel companies started by owning iron or coal assets, hence their regional locations in countries such as the UK, USA and Germany.

Much effort has gone into seeking to replicate this structural advantage through steel groups looking to invest into iron ore juniors, and similarly juniors have courted steel groups as cornerstone, strategic investors. Chinese producers in particular have pursued this approach also as a foil to the perceived power of the big three iron ore miners. The results for China have been lamentable, with upwards of $30 – $40 billion invested for little or no return. The causes of failure in this strategic thrust will be a subject for later. But a failure it has been so far.

Likewise consolidation was seen as a key to improved performance. This was expected to lead to more discipline in the management of capacity and a stabilisation of prices through the cycle. There have been some successes here, at least, on a geographical and product segment basis. Capacity has also been better managed through the current downturn through more flexible approaches to process management such as with blast furnaces. Overall on a global basis there has been little consolidation; this is largely because a period of substantial consolidation in the late 1990s and early part of the 2000s has been reversed by the emergence of a very fragmented Chinese steel industry.

Steel's underlying conundrum

A brief review of strategies employed to attack the underlying financial challenge shows that little impact has been made. All these strategies and others will be examined in greater depth in later chapters.

So here lies the challenge for the industry, its inherent conundrum: how can a product which is essential to all our lives and our standard of living, and that is almost infinitely flexible in form and use, not be produced in a way that is financially viable? For this is indeed the case. Furthermore, the use of steel will need to double, or even treble, in the next 40 years and will therefore require massive amounts of capital for investment. How can this be generated if the current investments show such a poor return?

This work will seek to demonstrate the existence of this conundrum and then to generate insight into the underlying causes of the industry's economic performance - and how to work to remove these conditions. In the process, I will show how the industry could develop over the next 50 years so it can continue to fulfil its role in our civilisation.

CHAPTER TWO

Steel and its discontents

"It's an old story. Yet somehow always new." Heinrich Heine

An unhappy industry

The growth story of steel so far would suggest a happy industry. Economic growth is sought after by individuals as it is helpful to achieving a good and happy life and the same applies to industries - all seek growth for numerous reasons, not least because it tends to make profitability and attracting capital easier. Steel, as we have seen, has been exceptionally successful in a range of ways. For long periods of time it has also experienced strong growth. During the entire 20th century demand grew faster than GDP as a whole. In other words, it outpaced the average of all other industries. During the period 1945-1973 growth was 6% p.a. and from 2000 through to now it has been stronger again, driven by China. However, as we saw towards the end of the last chapter, the industry is discontented, distressed and financially very unhappy, and this is true for most of the time. How can this be?

The purpose of any industry is to make society wealthier. Depending on the industry, there are all sorts of intermediate purposes: the products can do good; the services can be attractive; customer tastes and requirements can be met; but, if the sum total of societal wealth is not enhanced, an industry will wither and die through the disappearance of its customers and financial funders. The measure of health is given by looking to financial returns.

The returns generated are a function of the attractiveness of the products and services, their appeal to consumers and their willingness to pay for them, plus the efficiency with which the industry uses assets. If returns are poor – signaling unattractive products or inefficiency in operations - then investors will not reinvest and the assets will deteriorate, eventually ceasing to be productive. The industry will collapse into bankruptcy. It is that simple.

EXHIBIT 2.1: HISTORIC STEEL INDUSTRY ROCE AND EBIT MARGIN/%

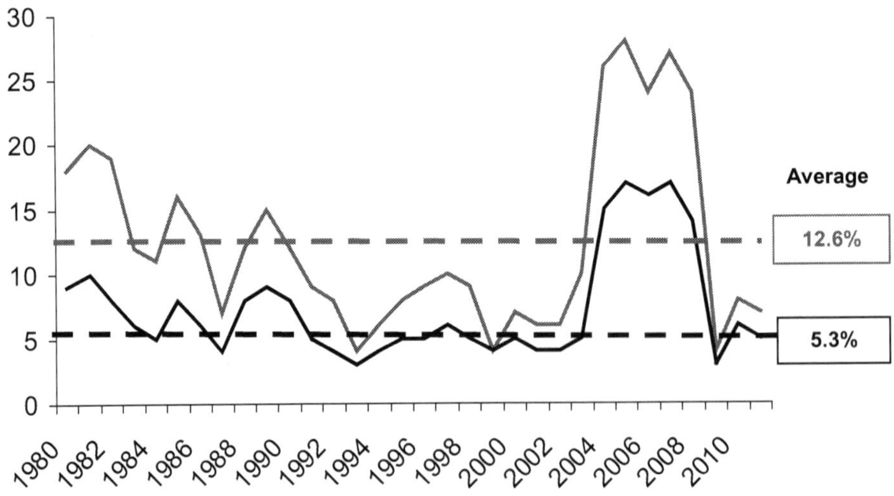

Source: BCG, worldsteel, Bloomberg and Hatch

The returns in steel are extremely poor. Exhibit 2.1 demonstrates that clearly. The Return on Capital employed (ROCE) in 2012 was 8.1% and the Earnings before Interest and Tax (EBIT) were less than 5%. Over the 32 years between 1980 and 2011 the ROCE averaged 12.6% and the EBIT averaged 5.3%. In the last 20 years these returns were only exceeded for the years 2003 to 2008. The average returns for these two metrics have deteriorated and for the last 20 years were lower than for the period as a whole.

A company has to use capital and the cost of this is called the Weighted Average Cost of Capital (WACC). The ROC can be compared to the WACC for, say, Nucor, the best regarded steel company in the USA: their WACC in 2013 was 7.6%. If the ROC is less than the WACC then the company is destroying value and itself. Nucor has one of the lowest WACC's in the industry due to its history of financial outperformance. The average WACC for the whole industry is much higher; but the returns for the average steel enterprise are much below their WACC. The industry is slowly going bankrupt.

EXHIBIT 2.2: HISTORIC STEEL INDUSTRY CASH FLOWS AND EBITDA / (US$/t)

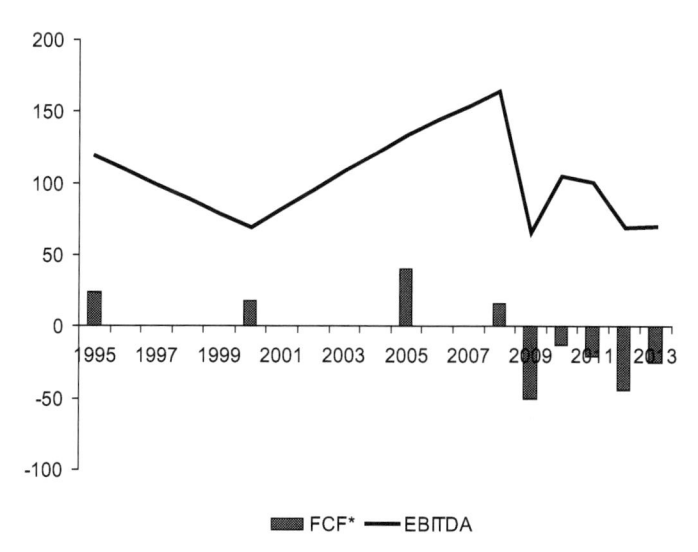

*Free cash Flow (FCF) = EBITDA – Interest Expense – Income taxes – Capital outlays;
Source: Source: Gerdau, WSD and Hatch

Another way of looking at this issue of returns is to look at Free Cash Flow (FCF). This is the amount of cash generated by the firm which is available for discretionary allocation; to shareholders, or for capital investment beyond maintenance capital for existing assets. Exhibit 2.2 provides a view on this as presented by Gerdau in 2013. The net position of the steel industry is negative for each of the last five years.

According to McKinsey, a respected consulting firm active in the steel sector, the required EBITDA for a self-sustainable economic equation in steel is between 17% and 18%. This is illustrated by them in Exhibit 2.3. I would endorse this view and it is clearly in excess of the industry's achievement. These analyses are of critical importance and I will examine why this is so crucial in later chapters when I look at the growth of the industry and the need for capital for investment.

EXIBIT 2.3: EBITDA REQUIRMENTS FOR THE STEE INDUSTRY

- Sustainable Net Debt/EBITDA: 2.5x
- Cost of debt: 8%
- Capital turnover (Rev./Invested Capital): 1.7
- Cost of equity: 10%

- Cost of debt: 20% of EBITDA
- Effective tax rate: 25% of EBITDA
- Cost of equity: 12% of EBITDA
- CAPEX: 7% of revenues
- R & D: 1 – 2% of revenues

Minimum EBITDA to sustain he industry: 17%

Source: McKinsey and WSD

Survival, capital markets and state intervention

This is not a new phenomenon. During the 25 years from 1974 to 1999 there were accumulated losses of over $200bn, according to the accounts of the steel companies which could be relied on to be accurate by international accounting standards. Indeed during this period and into the early 2000s, many steel companies did go bankrupt. In the US, LTV, Bethlehem Steel and others filed for Chapter 11 (creditor protection) and by 2002, for Chapter 7 (liquidation). In Europe, the British Steel Corporation was created in 1967 through nationalisation and lost a net $20-30bn before privatisation in 1988. The overwhelming majority of the French industry was taken into state ownership to avoid technical bankruptcy. The industries in Belgium, Italy, Sweden and Spain all had similar experiences. The governments of these countries poured tens of billions into the industry to support it through covering losses and providing capital for modernisation.

This state indulgence was a result of the employment importance of the industry allied to its structural importance for the rest of industry and society, a theme I covered in the previous chapter. In 1980 the British Steel Corporation employed about 300,000 people. Major economies in Europe could not contemplate the disruptions of liquidation and could not rely on imports so nationalisation, with the purpose of creating a period for reconstruction and improvement, was seen as the answer.

State ownership allowed for funds to be supplied which would not have been justified by returns and therefore were unavailable through normal financial markets. However in some jurisdictions, especially in the USA, state intervention through ownership was not politically acceptable. Here corporations had to survive as best they could. Trade barriers and anti-dumping actions helped, but the USA had been import-dependent since the disaster of the US Steel labour lock-out of 1959. This had forced users to import and allowed distributors and offshore suppliers to establish a major penetration, which has never been substantially dented.

Survival in the USA was supported by the liquidation of non-core assets. The big US steel groups in the 1950s and 1960s owned very substantial assets outside steelmaking. Bethlehem Steel had major shipyards, structural steel fabrication operations and stakes in a number of iron ore assets. US Steel was the largest owner of coal assets in the world and had stakes in many steel operations in Europe. US Steel had been the discoverer of the massive Carajas iron ore deposit in Brazil, but Brazilian regulatory barriers and internal politics had deprived it of the asset. The non-core assets were shed and the cash used to support the core and pay for the cost of closures and rationalisation.

Mass closures and Chapter 11, which provided for debts to be discounted or written off totally, together with occasional inputs of capital from the markets when prospects looked temporarily attractive, served to keep the industry afloat.

In the communist world these imperatives of returns and customers did not apply but the non-communist industries and markets were effectively cut off by trade restrictions and state dictat. Their poor product quality disbarred them from competing much in the non-communist markets. They existed in an autarkic economic state. These operations were shown to be massively financially dysfunctional when communism collapsed in 1990.

In the markets which have seen new steel industries emerge, such as Brazil and China, there has been subsidised capital and restricted market access to offshore product. In China, the central and provincial governments have paid little attention to capital efficiency. Steel was and is needed to construct a modern economy and the demand far exceeded any potential imports so it had to be made internally. It achieves little to bemoan this state of affairs – it was inevitable. The Chinese government admits that the future requires something better in financial terms and the Chinese people are regarded across S.E. Asia as being highly commercial, so change will come.

In Brazil the state again took a strong lead. The steel company CSN was state-owned from before World War II and was the first Brazilian integrated steel producer. Afterwards, the state investment corporation, Siderbras, was used as a vehicle to develop the country's iron ore and steel sectors. This developed the iron ore business which became CVRD, and now Vale, and a number of steel-producing assets, including what became Usiminas and other BF based integrated producers. Private companies were present and quite strong, including some foreign entities such as ARBED (Luxembourg) and Vallourec (France). Most private entities and all locally owned ones were in the EAF sector. The Brazilian sectors did not escape the financial issues. The privatisation of Siderbras resulted in revenues to the state of $5 bn, but the investment in cash over the years had been $25 bn.

Only India has managed without large amounts of state capital or subsidy. Here there was a state involvement through NMDC in iron ore and SAIL in steel. This remains the case but the state controls only some 25% of steel production. The private sector, however, has flourished, starting with Tata Steel but now incorporating a complex of companies and technologies. Whilst most have survived and expanded with financing both internal and external, it has not been without a quite remarkable degree of tolerance from the local banks. The conditions in India, however, seem to have helped the industry to flourish. It is a market quite difficult to penetrate with imports: there are local raw materials, much under the control of steel-makers, low cost and skilled labour and entrepreneurial management and ownership. There is a supportive relationship between family-controlled enterprises and the banks; a mutual commitment exists to "building the country".

So, except for a few years in the recent China-driven boom, returns have not led to an industry which is financially self-sustaining, with the possible exception of India representing a small 5% of world production. The ultimate funder over the last four decades has been the state – otherwise known as the tax payer, alias you and me, dear reader.

The self-diagnosis

It is to be expected that there would exist a self-diagnosis of the industry's ills. Indeed this is the case. It is also the case, in common with other subgroups in society, whether economic or social, that the diagnosis tends to identify the problems as largely external. Very little is perceived as the responsibility of, and within the power of, the group itself to change. This is usual but unfortunately not helpful. I believe that most of the difficulties can be found within the industry itself, which has the enormous benefit that they are within its own power to change. The self-identified causes, which are steel industry specific rather than generic issues, can be listed as:

- overcapacity; that is, an excess of productive capacity for steel making over market demand leading to unmanageable consequences for planning and to,
- price and volume volatility; that is, the propensity of prices and demand levels to rise and fall "excessively", causing unmanageable consequences for cash flow and profitability,
- excessively high raw materials costs; that is, a distortion in the market for raw materials which is somehow "unfair" and excessively rewards suppliers of those materials to the detriment of users who are unable to compensate for this in their market,
- unfair competition; this is, the perception that some producers have advantages over others due to their particular conditions either in terms of supply of capital or control of their local market,
- a lack of consolidation; that is, the absence of producers large enough to have a positive stabilising influence on the market and/or the introduction of new capacity, a condition which is believed to exist in other industrial sectors.

In the next chapter, I will explore the reality of these conditions, assess their true nature and, where there is reality, I will address the responses required in later chapters.

Exhibit 2.4 shows Gerdau's diagnosis of the steel industry's challenges, both generic and specific to its own circumstances.

EXHIBIT 2.4: GLOBAL SCENARIO CHALLENGES
- Overcapacity in the steel industry
- Exchange rate "War"
- Margin compression due to increasing costs
- Government policies (fiscal, monetary and tributary)
- State-owned enterprises
- International trade of steel intensive goods
- Unfair trade
- Threat to steel industry sustainability

Source: Gerdau and WSD (SSS Conference New York 2013)

CHAPTER THREE

The reality of the diagnosis

"Clear your mind of cant" Samuel Johnson

Overcapacity

Overcapacity is a frequently identified condition. Now, in 2014, it is the case as it was throughout the period from 1975 to 1999. In Europe, Eurofer, the European steel industry trade association, estimates the excess as between 40 and 50Mt or about 20% of capacity. Globally, estimates range from 300 to 500Mt. The variation is to be expected as the number changes with commissioning and decommissioning and actual capacity is difficult to determine given product mix variations, maintenance schedules and so on.

Excess capacity became so acute in the late 1970s in Europe that the emerging European Union (EU) declared a "manifest crisis". Under this declaration, the normal rules attaching to cartels and other market-limiting structures and actions did not apply. The habit of centrally regulated cartels had been long established as the industry came under the 1952 European Coal and Steel Community agreement. This became the founding institutional instrument of the current EU as a whole. This had deliberately regulated the industry because the competition between France and Germany over iron and coal in the Alsace-Lorraine and Ruhr regions was seen as a casus belli for the two world wars. A lateral-thinking mind might have seen this instrument as a cause of rather than solution to, the financial and capacity crisis of the industry – but lateral thinking is not always plentiful in the councils of Europe.

Europe decided to enforce a "voluntary", centrally driven reorganisation through the D'Avignon plan. Those producers joining the plan could receive EU-funded cash to facilitate restructuring. Enforcement of voluntarism was by the declaration of subsidies to members made outside the plan to be illegal. Only two significant steel groups elected to remain independent: the British Steel Corporation (UK) and Boel (Belgium). The plan allowed subsidies to be dispensed to producers with assets deemed lower cost and more competitive in order to modernise, consolidate and rationalise, whilst denying them to others, thus enforcing closure and bankruptcy.

Gross overcapacity, in the sense of simple excess of productive assets over inherent demand, was certainly the case. The oil price rise of 1973 had brought with it a period of lower growth in global economies. Annual global growth in crude steel slumped from 6% to 1%. Economies slowed and no new large centres of growth emerged. The impact of South Korea and Taiwan could not match the reindustrialisation of Germany and other parts of Western Europe after 1945, and the rise of Japan after the Korean War. The expectations following the rapid growth of 1945 to 1973 led to capacity overshoot. After all, it takes at least five years to build a major steel plant, and up to ten years when including the adjustment of planning expectations. Many plants were under development or being planned when the oil price shock occurred. In 1973 the British Steel Corporation was planning for a capacity of 33 Mt. Demand for its products in the UK never grew beyond 20Mt p.a. and export markets never met expectations.

Steel's success reinforced the difficulties

This decline in demand growth worldwide, from 6% p.a. to around 1%, was in crude steel. The capacity issue was compounded by other developments. Through yields, from liquid steel to the finished steel products, grew greatly in the 1974-1999 period. Many new developments happened in steelmaking and processing technology during this period. Yield increases in steelmaking were facilitated by a most important innovation - continuous casting, which replaced batch based ingot casting. This in itself improved the through yield by over 10%. Other developments such as the almost total replacement of open hearth furnaces (OHF) by basic oxygen furnaces (BOF), at least outside the communist countries, and the integration of discrete processes into continuous processes, especially by automation, also meant that a given volume of crude steel made an increased volume of finished steel.

The adoption of these changes was driven by the search for improved performance. The absence of gross volume growth focused steel-makers on improvements in efficiency, which all the above represented. This success did not alleviate the problem of capacity, rather it compounded it. The numbers were very significant. Experience then and now, is that "capacity creep" occurs in large-scale integrated steel plants. Every time maintenance is conducted and assets are renewed, capacity increases. The human being finds better ways of doing things as a matter of routine if motivated to do so. During this time, efficiency improvements reinforced this capacity creep phenomenon. The evidence suggests that this creep amounts to over 1% p.a. This needs to be added to the 10% improvement due to the one-off installation of continuous casting. Over a 25-year period (1974-1999) these dynamics resulted in about a 30% improvement in efficiency of through yield from raw materials to finished steel. This is illustrated by Exhibit 1.3 showing the improvement over this period in yield between crude steel and finished steel for the German steel industry.

This was not all. Steel users also were under pressure. The automobile industry was downsizing its vehicles. All manufacturers of metal products were seeking improvements in their yield from purchased material and looking for lighter, better, longer-lasting and corrosion-resistant steels. As usual, steel was highly successful in meeting these demands. Unfortunately, everywhere manufacturing improvements in the use of steel took place, the capacity issue was reinforced. Steel was making this problem more intractable by its very successes.

Overcapacity today

The situation of overcapacity now is rather different from that of 1974-1999. Growth in demand is still there and the efficiency gains of the previous period cannot be replicated. Capacity creep can occur but there are no obvious one-off gains such as continuous casting, or BOFs replacing OHFs. The overshoot in capacity, driven as before by excessive optimism in expectations of demand, will neither be long lasting nor exacerbated by the yield improvement dynamics of the 1970s and 80s. The overcapacity problem today will be temporary given underlying global growth in demand is not 1% but between 3% and 4%. The boom of the mid 2000s led to over- enthusiasm. China in particular can be seen to have a surplus of crude capacity, even if only temporarily as its industrialisation still has a long way to go. China's drive for capital productivity is just beginning, increasingly required as the labour force matures and faces the start of a decline. This will involve large-scale rationalisation of inefficient and subscale capacities.

The calls for outside assistance to help with this perceived problem are misplaced; the pace of action by the public sector is such that actions if taken will emerge too late and they will have unforeseen consequences which are better avoided. The problem for producers is by no means as severe as in earlier decades. Neither in Europe nor North America has a major producer gone bankrupt in the current extended downturn. There is no need for governmental or quasi-governmental assistance, perhaps another D'Avignon plan, or other forms of state subsidy, re-nationalisation or trade barriers. The institutional memory of the sector, which drives the demands for state action, runs deep but these are siren calls.

Fortunately the political importance of the steel sector is much reduced and so politicians will find it easy to avoid responding to these siren voices. In the developed world the steel sector is no longer a major employer. Tata Steel in the UK, the successor to British Steel, now employs only about 20,000 people. Steel is not a politically sensitive industry in the developed economies as it is in developing economies. Development cannot take place without steel and history shows that foreign capacities cannot fill this need for major centres of population, such as China and India. This may change, as smaller countries become more prominent in economic development, as we will discuss later.

Most importantly, consolidation and the withdrawal of the state have bred more responsibility in the use of capacities, avoiding downward price spirals. In addition, producers have learnt new measures to make production more flexible. There has been a big improvement in the producers ability to withstand periods of overcapacity and much more can be done as will be shown.

Steel companies can be likened to a convoy. A convoy travels at the speed of the slowest ship. In the great convoy of economic life the slowest ships are bureaucracies and the slowest of these are public sector ones. Though strong, the appeal of state support or intervention should be resisted. It is hard to find a case where industrial economic adjustments were assisted by direct government intervention. Political goals may of necessity override economic ones, but economic adjustment is hindered every time by intervention. Support, if it is to be provided, is best done through contextual motivational tools such as tax breaks for closure costs, or a holiday from punitive new taxes such as carbon taxes. There are many ways to do this. The D'Avignon plan may have been a political necessity but hindsight would suggest it was not a financial or economic success.

Misunderstanding overcapacity

Beyond all these considerations is a much greater one, for overcapacity can easily be misunderstood. In any mature industry there is seldom a match between productive capacity and actual demand. Indeed, this can be likened to the metaphor of the broken clock: such a clock shows the right time, but only twice a day, only 2 minutes out of every 1,440 to be exact. So it is with capacity and demand in relation to the economic cycle: they match each other only occasionally. A mature industry has established technologies which are easily available to purchase and not predominantly protected by restrictive patents; an extensive cadre of experienced managers who are mobile; customers who are many and knowledgeable as to the product's use; and capital markets which are familiar with the industry and able to assess risks and returns: these factors certainly describe the steel sector.

Such an industry, especially when subject to clear and large cycles as this one is, will find that capacity nearly always exceeds demand. For if it does not, then prices will escalate, expected returns will likewise follow and producers will seize the perceived opportunity to build new capacity. Given the planning and construction lead times involved, this capacity will be commissioned mostly during subsequent down cycles, thus giving rise to excess capacity, but this will be absorbed by the next upturn. There is a naturally self-correcting process at work here. The amount of such natural and expected excess capacity in the down times can be estimated at 15%. When "overcapacity" is less than approximately 15%, there occurs an upward and unsustainable surge in prices as producers fail to actually produce at higher than 90% of stated capacity for any extended period. This is what happened in the period 2006/7 when hot rolled coil (HRC) prices worldwide exceeded

$1,100 /t. during this surge "overcapacity" was never considered to be less than 18%.

What executives should be concentrating on is how to manage this pattern better. The responsibility is theirs and to wish for anything else is to cry for the moon. In fact they have been doing this by such technical efforts as making the operations of blast furnaces, the most rigid of the stages in the production process, capable of being operated on a more flexible basis. There have been big improvements here, but there is much more to do and in other parts of the business model, most particularly in managing the revenue consequences of volatility.

It is the management of capacity, not its defined amount and relation to demand which is the challenge. The state should only focus on avoiding barriers to the exit of capacity, not on the management of capacity as such. Facilitation, not intervention, is as always the preferred option for state interventions if the objective is a healthy industry.

Volatility

Volatility is built into economic process. The abolition of boom and bust was, is and will remain a fantasy, although much desired by people with orderly minds. Rationalists and progressives will seek the abolition of boom and bust; empiricists and conservatives will learn to live with it, aiming to mitigate its consequences. Politicians sometimes speak of achieving the rationalists' ambition of abolition but we should always beware of the imminent arrival of crisis. Thus Alan Greenspan, Chairman of the US Federal Reserve from 1987-2006, spoke of the "Goldilocks economy", not too hot or too cold, which turned out to be a furnace of financial destruction, and Gordon Brown, UK Chancellor of the Exchequer and later Prime Minister, claimed the glory for the abolition of boom and bust. Hubris is always present in anyone in the public domain; history looks unkindly on those who seek cheap populist applause by promising the impossible; nemesis will follow soon after.

All politicians succumb to hubris if lasting long enough; good political judgment lies in embracing hubris as late as possible.

Like hubris in politicians, volatility in economies is inevitable; what matters is how you deal with it. In steel, volatility in both volumes and prices can be quite extreme. Steel production stands almost at the beginning of the value chain for economic activity and if mining is taken into account then, indeed, at the very beginning. As economic activity turns, expectations change. Businesses find it difficult to plan for anything other than continuity. The impacts of the cycle on steel demand can be seen through a simple example.

I will use the traditional tool of the philosopher - a thought experiment. Imagine a component supplier for some basic manufactured product where steel is a major element of their manufacturing process. In classic economic cases, the example is often called a widget-maker. The steel market is made up of such customers: small to medium-sized producers of things - tubes, stampings, forgings, profiles, wire, etc, maybe 50 million of them. For these enterprises, steel is 60-70% of their total cost. Their ordering pattern for steel will be set to an expectation of continuity. When the economy turns, this expectation ends and the demand for their products, and their expectations of suppliers, turn up or down. They respond by expanding or shrinking orders from suppliers, including the steel producer. This is compounded by the need to hold inventories.

At an annual volume of 100 widgets they may hold 3 months' raw material inventory, which is steel for 25 units. Now, if the economy turns up, then next month's orders for widgets may go to ten instead of eight. This implies expectations of annual demand of 120. The enterprise's expectations are changed and with them its ordering pattern to its steel suppliers. If volumes are seen to be 120 then 3 months' inventory is 30. It will also be expected that inventories will be expended more quickly through increased production and the delay in replenishment. By the time the steel company responds after, say, one month, the firm will be down to 1.5 months of inventory at the new level. This is steel for only 15 units, so it expects to need 15 units worth of steel to build up to a required level. Orders are placed on steel suppliers to that effect.

The steel company sees a swing from orders of eight per month to 15, a growth of nearly 100%. This compounding occurs through the entire value chain and in ups or downs. Hence the cycle is extraordinarily enhanced at the start of the value chain: either up or down. This process can be even more dramatic if, as sometimes happens, the component supplier decides to be extra cautious. If he has been disappointed in his main steel company in the past, he might duplicate his order with a second steel company.

When the economic cycle changes, it is common for demand for end products bought by end users, the purchasing of automobiles for instance, to grow or decline by 5% in a month. It is easy to envisage how this can result in a perceived change of 15% for steel.

This volatility also affects pricing behaviour. Pricing is the market's means of rationing. Faced with a slump in demand the steel company will have two anxieties. The first is that it will be left holding excess inventories and will require increased working capital, which will be needed at a time of reduced expectations generally. Banks are going to be tougher in these times and steel companies generally have weak balance sheets so this exposure is something to be avoided if possible. The second anxiety is the loss of market share. This might result if competitors, facing the same circumstances, seek to offload their inventories and capacity through low pricing. This is more likely to happen in markets which will not contaminate the second company's normal market - hence, in someone else's "backyard".

In an upturn, product supply can be rationed by pricing. The steel company, having suffered excessively in the downturn, needs to rebuild its cash flow, reduce the increased working capital it had to take on and enhance its profitability. The temptation to raise prices "excessively", in the view of the customer, is almost irresistible.

It cannot be denied that all the circumstances of the business cycle lead to volatility, and that it is at its most extreme for upstream industries such as steel. Exhibit 3.1 provides charts showing the volatility for certain product prices in N. Europe and USA against the price of scrap and iron ore. I will examine later how this situation can be better managed, but calls for restraint amongst competitors are fruitless, as is the call for stabilisation of prices from suppliers. All must act in their perceived best interest – but this can be radically transformed by better and more timely, information.

EXHIBIT 3.1: STEEL, SCRAP AND IRON ORE PRICES (US$/t and US$/dmt)

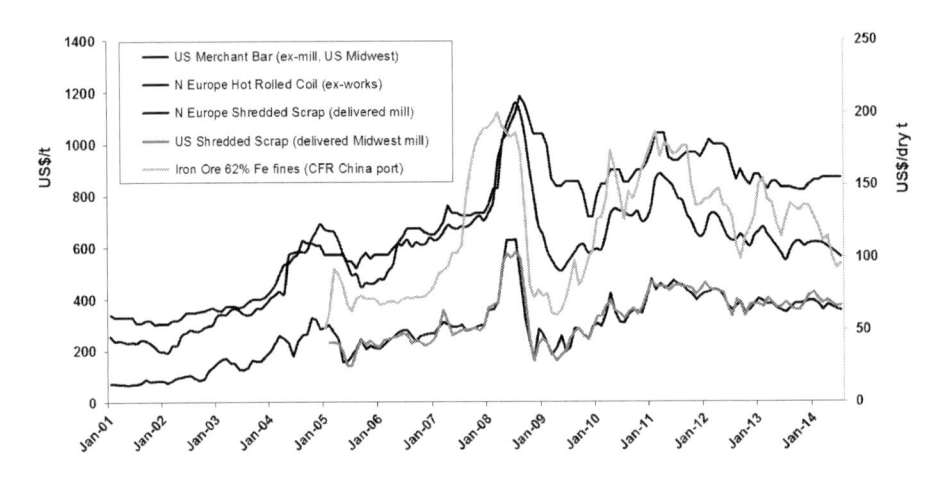

Source: The Steel Index (TSI) and Platts

Raw materials and steel margins

The relation between suppliers and users of raw materials has changed in the last decade, to the detriment of the users – the steel companies. Iron ore suppliers in particular have increased their prices substantially. The chart here, Exhibit 3.2, shows two things: the rise in iron ore prices for the last 10 years and the fall in real terms that had existed in the years before. Metallurgical coal prices have also risen.

Here, though there is the opportunity for substitution with lower grades of hard coking coal, such as pulverised coal injection (PCI), and for direct reduced iron (DRI) rather than pig iron. So, competition serves to moderate these prices. Iron ore is not amenable to substitution except in the long term by scrap and EAF production. This is, however, a later stage phenomenon when steel use in a location is already high. Scrap is, in origin, virgin iron ore.

EXHIBIT 3.2: REAL ANNUAL IRON ORE PRICES 1968-2012 (Australian Fines FOB 2012 US$/DMt)

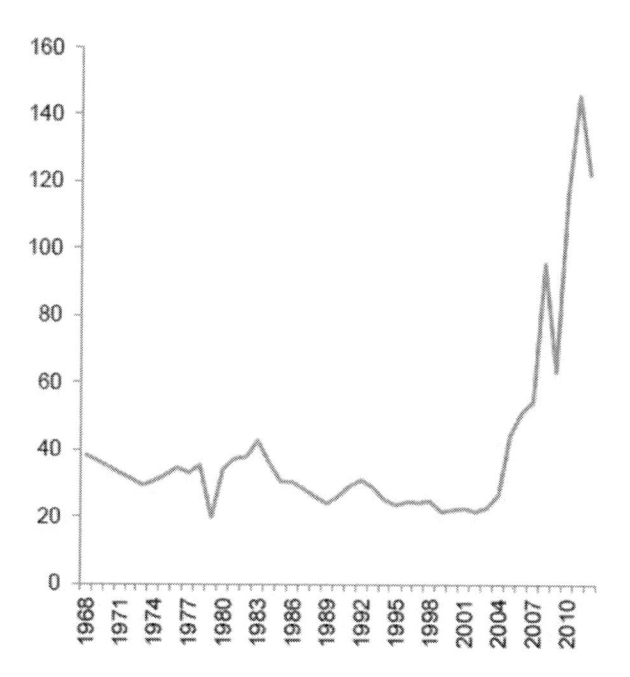

Source: ABARE/BREE and Hatch

Virgin ore will be the predominant source of iron for the next 50 years, after that scrap will become the dominant material. Do high raw material prices constitute a problem? A look at Exhibit 3.1 will demonstrate that when raw material prices are high, in fact, steel margins tend to widen.

The cost structure for steelmaking has changed over the last decade. Using the BF route and primary raw materials, the manufacture of one tonne of steel requires about 1.6 tonnes of iron ore and 550kg of coke, equivalent to about a tonne of hard coking coal. These numbers can be reduced, as scrap can be used in the BOF, in practice up to 25% of the charge. Coke use can also be reduced by using PCI. However, for this little example, a basic mix is assumed. Other raw materials such as ferro-alloys can be ignored, at least for carbon steels. I shall also ignore the cost of transport.

Back in the 1990s when ore was $20 /t and metallurgical coal $60 /t then the raw materials cost only $92 /t of crude steel. In the worst pricing environment, the spot price for hot rolled coil was never lower than $300 /t so steel -makers were still left with twice the cost of raw materials available for covering other costs and providing a margin. Furthermore, the working capital requirements were also low. If three months' worth of raw material was required to be funded, then for a 4Mt p.a. steel site only $92M of working capital was required for iron ore and coal.

All this has changed. Now raw material prices are higher and that has led to higher steel prices. Raw material costs are now approximately $130 /t for iron ore and $175 /t for metallurgical coal, thus for the basic mix they are a total of $383 /t of crude steel. However the spot price for hot rolled coil is now $590 /t in NW Europe (as of August 2013). The market environment is very similar to when the spread - the difference between the scrap price and the hot rolled price - was $208 back in 2001 and is again at $208. Steel companies have not benefitted as raw material suppliers have, and working capital requirements are very substantially higher than back in 2001. For three months they are now $383M as opposed to $92M. Given that operating costs such as consumables, labour and energy have also risen; margins have been squeezed.

The making of standard steel grades to the hot rolled stage is looking very much like a low value-adding processing activity with little room for differentiation and margin enhancement. The balance of revenue, and margin, opportunity has definitely switched to the raw material suppliers. This can be seen clearly in Exhibit 3.1. Here is shown the spread between scrap and HRC in Northern Europe. The price of scrap closely follows the price of pig iron which closely follows the price of raw materials to make the iron. So it is a good surrogate for the cost structure of all steel-makers. Whilst the surge in HRC prices in the middle of the decade enhanced the spread available to steel companies, its recent decline has left the scrap price structurally higher and the spread back to approximately what it was, at least for HRC in northern Europe.

In economist's jargon, the terms of trade have moved to the detriment of steel-makers. It is irrelevant and unhelpful to talk of whether this is fair or unfair; rather it is worth examining to see if this is something that can be reversed or mitigated for the industry. This I will do in a later chapter. Suffice it to acknowledge here that the movement in the terms of trade does constitute a challenge: working capital demands are much greater; there appears to have been no enhancement to their, the steel makers, spreads, indeed with inflation in processing costs, they have deteriorated. Without some change elsewhere, basic steelmaking is no longer a business with opportunities for profit above the cost of capital.

Unfair competition

State intervention in the provision of capital is still widespread in the industry. This is obvious in China but is also present elsewhere. In Europe, SSAB/Ruukki, voestalpine, Salzgitter, Dillinger Hutte and Saarstahl in carbon steel and Outokumpu in stainless, all have major blocks of shares in state hands. Outside Europe, companies in many developing countries have state involvement in their share structures. There was a time around 1990 when 50% of the world steel capacity could be said to be under the control of governments. This percentage rapidly declined with the wave of privatisation which occurred in Western Europe and then in Russia, the Ukraine and Brazil. It looked like the days of state involvement were nearly dead and the percentage of capacity wholly or partially in state hands became as low as maybe 10-15%. The growth of the Chinese steel industry, largely with state funds, has reversed this trend and we are probably back to around 50% state ownership. There is no doubt that state involvement can and does distort competition. This functions both directly and indirectly through a distortion of expectations.

The direct effect is that those who don't have to pay for capital, which equates to capacity, are careless in its use. As humans, what we don't pay for we don't value. Certainly the provision of "free" capital encourages pricing at below cost in the downturns. The cost of closures and the idling of capacity are real challenges for managers in none state owned companies who have to deal with unhappy workers and communities and irate shareholders; whilst the challenge of losses to managers in state owned companies is much less so as it creates only explanatory requirements to administrators and politicians who have a hundred other agenda items and short attention spans. This behaviour is detrimental to the interests of the shareholders of privately owned producers. Even if the behaviour is closely monitored and there are penalties for companies operating at below cost with subsidy – which is true in the European cases – there is a degree of asymmetric competition. The producers relying on private shareholders know they will be less forthcoming of capital than the state and so they have to be more guarded in their competitive behaviour. They will tend to compete in parts of the market away from those occupied by the state-owned companies. This will restrict their success and lead to poorer service for customers. This distortion is one of expectations, but no less detrimental than unfair price competition even if more opaque.

It is possible to see a future of much-reduced state ownership. The Chinese phenomenon is unique. India, which has a population about to exceed China's, has managed to produce a thriving steel sector with minimal state ownership, showing that it is possible to industrialise a large country without massive state involvement. In the Chinese case, the commitment to speed of growth based on steel-intensive investment did require volumes of steel which could not be supplied by imports or local entrepreneurial ventures, restricted, as they were, in their access to capital.

The next wave of industrialisation, outside the BRIC countries (Brazil, Russia, India and China) will be in countries of smaller populations and ones with a very varied set of circumstances. I shall discuss this later in the chapter on medium-term growth, but for now it is enough to say that I believe these countries will be satisfied as to their steel demand without large-scale state involvement. I shall demonstrate why this can be the case. There is a major opportunity for established private-sector steel producers, if and when, they can justify access to new capital. We should also expect the Chinese industry to privatise and the government there to manage its investments better through the next cycle. China needs productive assets, not just producing assets, to meet their future economic requirements. They have an aging population which will require much increased social spending and the pressure to create employment is already subsiding, to be replaced with pressure for better returns.

Lack of consolidation

The sector is perceived to be fragmented. The largest steel company is ArcelorMittal which represents approximately 8% of global crude steel capacity. The next largest company is only 4% of capacity. There are many hundreds of steel-makers in the world; hundreds in China alone. By contrast, in iron ore, the seaborne trade is dominated by three companies which hold about 65% of the market share. If all ore production is included, then they have about 43%. The largest has over 20%. By comparison, in stainless steel the largest company has about 10% and the largest five companies represent about 30%. In aluminium, the largest producer is approximately 10% of capacity. So in other materials the degree of consolidation is about the same as steel. It does not appear that consolidation is less than in other relevant sectors. Indeed if we look at the numbers on a segmental basis, steel can look very consolidated.

Not all steel is the same and competition is restricted by geographical accessibility and product qualities. Geography and market sector analyses of consolidation show a variable picture compared to total gross capacity numbers. In Europe, ArcelorMittal holds about 35% of the flat rolled sector. Indeed this is the degree of control which the EU competition authorities use as the threshold before consolidation is regarded as distorting competition and capacity shedding is required. Steel supply for the automotive sector in particular is restricted by quality and service considerations. Automotive assemblers require just-in-time performance which is a big barrier to entry for suppliers; as a result, steel supply to this sector is more consolidated than automotive assembly itself on a continental basis. The sector is limited to a half dozen major suppliers of flat rolled product.

Even more demanding is the supply of high quality grain oriented electrical steels which in the world is limited, again, to half a dozen suppliers.

The pattern of consolidation by product in Europe is mimicked in North America where it is even higher in commodity long products with two producers representing about 70% of local supply. If we look at spreads for hot rolled bar products over scrap in North America the average spreads have widened over the period of 15 years and this widening is coincidental with the large consolidation which occurred in 2000-2005. Indeed, spreads have increased by $100 /t. This is a major increase in margin opportunity. So whilst raw material price movements appear to have narrowed margins, as explained above, consolidation has definitely widened them.

In Japan, Brazil and Russia - and even in India - many of the same characteristics apply. There are many sectors which are effectively much more consolidated than total crude capacity numbers would indicate. Admittedly, many of the sectors with high consolidation are small - the amount of grain oriented electrical steel in total is less than 0.5% of total steel demand - but automotive sheet demand is about 10%. However, much of steel is of a commodity nature and lack of consolidation is said to hamper profitability as it makes understanding of the market opaque and the ability of any individual producer to "stabilise" market dynamics to match available capacity difficult. There is much truth in this observation.

A higher level of consolidation would make market signalling easier and more effective but international consolidation will also serve to defuse the political importance of steel. One of the factors which has hindered good financial performance over decades has been the intervention of governments in mostly futile attempts to protect their indigenous steel producers. Multi-national group such as ArcelorMittal provide a means of explaining to governments the realities of comparative advantage and the relative competitiveness of different assets. This is of critical importance when difficult decisions on capacity closure need to be taken.

All producers will benefit from more consolidation in this way. Over the next 10-20 years I believe we will see a number of global groups emerge to match ArcelorMittal. The leading candidates for such a role are Korea's POSCO and the Japanese producers. They have many footholds in other markets than their home ones and are strong financially and technically. Perhaps an Indian producer, also Gerdau from Brazil could join this process. An interesting possibility is Nucor which alone among the North American producers has the capability to join this process. Indeed they may need to do so as their position in their home market is close to competitive limits.

Along the way to greater consolidation and globalisation, it is important to make good decisions. The effect of bad decisions is seen at ThyssenKrupp (TK). A decade ago this was seen as a possible globaliser and it had some strong positions outside Europe. However, the decision to invest over $10bn in a strategy to produce slabs in Brazil and coil in North America has led to massive write offs and the probable withdrawal of TK from full ownership of its European steel business . The fact that clear thinking could see the strategy was flawed just makes the result depressing.

A key to achieving globalisation is to buy, and invest, at the right time; when the prices of assets are realistic.

Conclusion

Steel is an unhappy industry. Its discontents are intense due to its inability to find a stable economic equation which will provide for adequate returns to satisfy private capitalist shareholders over the economic cycle. In this chapter, I have sought to examine the industry's diagnosis of this failure and pass comment on the validity of the theories. The major item in the diagnosis to which I shall return is volatility. Overcapacity is to my mind a red herring. Raw material prices are outside the industry's control and I will show how these might evolve later. State intervention, and its follower, unfair competition, will be addressed when I examine how the next wave of industrialising countries will satisfy their need for steel – and the state's role will be modest – if the steel companies can seize the opportunity available to them. There is one major point of diagnosis which the industry does not mention which is customer service. Here is a missing piece of the formula for contentment in steel and I will address that at some length.

By finding new ways to manage volatility, responding to the needs of emerging market demand in an innovative way, and focusing on service, the steel industry can find a path to contentment and long-term financial viability.

CHAPTER FOUR

Forecasting and its discontents

> *"In preparing for battle I have always found that plans are useless but planning is indispensable."* Dwight D Eisenhower

This book is about both the current, although continually recurring, challenges of the steel industry, and the short and long-term future prospects for this industry. How we should approach the exciting but fraught difficulties of forecasting is the subject of this chapter.

Forecasting as a branch of history

I have always been impressed by the inappropriateness of images purporting to represent people "looking into the future". Many will be familiar with the famous picture of Marianne leading the sans-culottes over the barricades during the French revolution, while striding powerfully forward into the future. Exhibit 4.1 is Delacroix's painting of this famous mythical character.

We always visualise the future as something we march forward into, as though we could see into it. In fact, we can only envisage the future, if at all, by looking into the past. We have hindsight not foresight, memory not clairvoyance. What we envisage as we think of the future is based only on what we remember of the past, not even the past itself. To my mind, the most appropriate way of visualising this is to see ourselves stumbling blindfold, backwards, into the future. This is not how our forecasters or our leaders like to portray themselves, so this is not how it is presented. Perhaps "blindfolded" is too harsh. After all, we look at the past and must base our views of the future on that, but we interpret, modify, adapt and filter our speculations about the future based on an attempt to learn. George Santayana, the Spanish philosopher's comment is apposite: "Those who do not learn from the past are condemned to repeat it"; and as Churchill added "first as farce and later as tragedy." Steel is in danger of such repetition. To borrow from Yogi Berra, steel tends towards having "déjà vu – all over again".

EXHIBIT 4.1: MARIANNE LEADING THE SANS CULOTTES OVER THE BARRICADES

The tools of the forecaster

Our tools for interpretation are essentially poetic and literary, involving metaphor and analogy. I use the word "essentially" judiciously as metaphors and analogies come first before any scientific tools. Only when we have a basic intellectual structure of drivers of change and their interdependence can we use models and other scientific approaches. This basic structure comes from analogy and metaphor. The current vogue for computer-based modelling pretends to escape from this and be more "scientific", forgetting the fact that science itself progresses by imaginative leaps of analogy. Today, claiming science as our authority induces religious devotion. This is very dangerous, because the practical power of science and its derivative, technology, is infinitely greater than religion.

Forecasters are the last people to wish to dispel their aura of superior insight. They have their own self-esteem and self-interest to protect. It is wise to take seriously the comments of Warren Buffett who is fond of saying that a forecast tells us more about the forecaster than about the forecasted. I heartily support this observation. Who would argue in the field of practical economics with the sage of Omaha?

Pretended omniscience is today the precondition for leadership, especially for a politician. Maybe it always was so; although reading Thucydides suggests it was different in classical Greece. How disconcerted might we feel if a leader were to seek our votes at an election on the basis that he stumbled better than his opponent? But such is the reality. We should take note of another comment from Nils Bohr when asked about forecasting: "Prediction is always difficult; especially when it is about the future. " He clearly understood the distorting lenses we wear when we attempt this most enticing but dangerous of tasks.

As metaphors and analogies are to creative writing, so our preconceptions, prejudices or biases regarding the future are to forecasting. Mine provide the foundations for my comments about the future of the ferrous sector.

Uncertainty, Heisenberg and forecasts

Forecasters are always wrong – but that does not invalidate their efforts, although it should temper our appreciation of them. Failure, or inaccuracy, is inevitable for two inescapable reasons: the above-mentioned stumbling, and the occurrence of unforeseen events. Even with perfect recollection of the past and the best use of judgment, there will be unforeseen and unforeseeable events. Indeed forecasting about economic and social issues is surely the perfect demonstration of Heisenberg's uncertainty principle (or more strictly speaking, observer principle) that when we look at something it induces change. When we communicate a forecast about any societal subject, such as economics, somebody will react to it and thus change the thing forecasted about. If economic and social forecasts are not meant as attempts to influence action and so change events, what are they meant for?

If we examine the nice graphs we are presented with showing trends for the future - economic growth or climatic temperature changes are perhaps the two most common today - we may be struck by their failure to show discontinuities. This cannot be otherwise. They will show variations, cycles, and a degree even of turbulence, but unforeseen discontinuities just cannot be forecast. The idea is an oxymoron: what is unforeseen cannot be forecasted. Yet unforeseen events will happen. Even if we seek to consider these as scenarios - "what will happen if …" - these situations must inevitably mimic those we recollect from the past. Wild surmises just would not carry credibility, but they will come to pass.

When Columbus sailed west from Cadiz he did not foresee meeting the Americas. This event changed the world in unforeseen ways. He thought he was sailing to find a new alternative route to India and China and was ridiculed by many who regarded the earth as flat. He believed that it was round but even this audacious speculation, radical as it was, was insufficient to predict what he would find. Was it possible to envisage the arrival of AIDS, the discovery of antibiotics, the construction of the wheel? I do not think so. So when we look backwards into the future through our partial and selective memory, even with the richest metaphors and analogies to assist, we would be wise to reflect on these conditioning factors. Yet we must consider how the future will emerge and develop. I prefer to think of this as envisaging the future rather than forecasting it.

I have myself spent a great part of my life envisaging the future, especially the future of the ferrous world. This is the subject of this chapter and the next two. This chapter will focus on the key assumptions and conditioning factors without which I find it impossible to envision at all. The next two chapters will focus on the specific possibilities.

The understandings without which nothing can be envisaged

Before immersing ourselves in this specific topic I will provide a series of basic assumptions which govern my thinking about the future: these are a series of what I consider "inevitabilities". In particular that:
- economic growth will remain the predominant human ambition for the foreseeable future
- human beings will continue to seek improved living standards
- technology will continue to evolve and will remain the mechanism whereby humans adapt to the external world
- humans will continue to aspire to personal freedom

It appears to me that without these assumptions then no forecasting of anything can even be attempted. A little explanation of each of these is in order.

The origins of economic growth

Economic growth has not always been a driving ambition of humans. For millennia it came as a by-product, if it came at all - which for most of the time it did not. Humans focused on survival. As hunter-gatherers, the possibility of economic development was only minimal. The constant movement of population following migrating herds of game inhibited the accumulation of knowledge, which requires record-keeping, and capital, which is knowledge made physical. These require a settled existence. This first became possible with the arrival of agrarian subsistence. Sometime around 10,000 years ago people in the Mesopotamian and Yangtze deltas first planted seeds deliberately and started to develop wheat and other cereal crops: oats may have been the first, thus demonstrating the early and continuing superiority of the Scots! Fascinatingly, these early farmers seem to have appeared in these two locations independently of each other and shortly after the last Ice Age.

The arrival of farming was possibly due to the benign influence of rising temperatures which have made life more tolerable and food resources more plentiful over the millennia. This is most clearly demonstrated in the two periods where we have reliable records: the Roman and Medieval warmings of Western Europe. The former facilitated Roman civilisation, involving the widespread establishment of the rule of law beyond the small scale city state as with the Greeks, for the first time, along with towns and trade. The latter made agriculture more productive with bigger and better harvests and so freed labour and enabled the building of the great cathedrals and the first early glimmers of industrialisation in the form of the guilds and trades of medieval cities.

A physically settled existence is required for agriculture – crops don't move and so humans have to stop moving also. The direct consumption of crops by humans is more ergonomically efficient than via the intermediation of animals, so surpluses in food availability released labour for activities other than agriculture. This led to specialisation, trade and thus the accumulation of capital. In parallel with these technical developments came the rule of law. Agriculture requires cultivation of land and no one is motivated to do this unless the ownership of the land and thus the crop is protected in enforceable law. A strong civil legal system, independent of any individual ruler, providing for the regulation of commerce and rights of ownership, is a vital requirement. Agriculture, civil society, settled populations in growing urban clusters, and the accumulation of capital, are all necessary to take man from hunter-gatherers to today's level of civilisation. Thus it can be argued that the origins of western civilisation lie not only in despotically ruled Mesopotamia, but also in Greece where the law transcended any individual.

Economic growth took root and, no doubt, became a subject for unrecorded debate. However, even then, other priorities, such as the search for security with settled borders, took precedence. In Europe it was not until the Renaissance and then the Reformation led to the triumph of the secular over the religious, that intellectual attention was freed to focus on wealth creation. The most important event in this process was probably the Peace of Westphalia, in 1648, which ended the Thirty Years War. These treaties established that the prince of a territory, its secular ruler, could determine the territory's religion and not vice versa. In fact, it established the primacy of the sovereign state and their rulers as the basis of secular authority. This bifurcation has still to take place in some non-western parts of the globe; most notably in the countries dominated by Islam.

For another two or three hundred years, the priority in the secular world, even in the west, was on the political, with economics being very subservient. Thus, we have the ideas of mercantilism and "Charter Capitalism", which placed industry and trade as instruments of public policy, rather than public policy as a facilitator of the former. The independence of economics and its transcendence in human priorities began with, and was most effectively represented by, Adam Smith's The Wealth of Nations (1776).

The ascendancy of economic growth

Since the late 18th century economics has become an intellectual discipline of its own and the understanding of how to achieve economic growth has itself grown immeasurably. I am not asserting that this now represents the only or even the dominant aim of political life. The dominant aim remains the achievement and retention of power by the competing political elites; it is impossible to see how this can be avoided. However, the predominant language of political discourse in democratic societies is now economic growth and well-being. All politicians promise this nirvana. Unfortunately, the achievement of growth is not always forthcoming: these elites have intellectual and historical commitments which inhibit their clear perception of reality and, thus, the achievement of what they espouse. This limitation can be seen everywhere in public policy debate and action, although we hope that it declines over generations.

All human beings have the failings of pride, hubris and self-regard which hinder their vision. Nearly every government espouses economic growth as their objective; but for a large part of their time, they fail to acknowledge the means of how to achieve it. Fortunately, in democratic societies the electorate has the periodic option of "throwing the rascals out" which in the game of power is the sanction which does lead to periodic bouts of wisdom. At root, it is this human condition of the limits to learning, and the inevitability of hubris, which causes economic cycles and volatility. However, it is the rise of democracy which encourages a belief in the inevitability of continuing economic growth.

I assume that for the foreseeable future economic growth and its benefits will remain the dominant objective of politics and despite politicians and their limitations, it will be achieved. There have been attempts to revive alternatives even in the West during the 19th and 20th centuries. The most pernicious of these attempts was communism, which wreaked havoc with human happiness for most of the 20th century. It took Russia from being the fourth-most industrialised nation in 1914 to no better than 20th in 1989. Thankfully, this is now extinguished although, unfortunately, it can still be troubling through its fellow-travelling intellectual dogmas of socialism and progressive liberalism. In all directions, the pursuit of secular wealth, whilst still to experience some setbacks and delays, will achieve the dominant position. In its favour, it does have the benefits of reducing disease, extending life, providing food and securing a better future for our children. These are not unattractive results.

Growth is required by the emerging population crisis

Finally, growth is the only way of dealing with the coming population crisis. This is not the crisis of popular fantasy, involving a population too large for the planet to support. That is Malthusianism rewritten for the 21st century. The real crisis is the one of an ageing population. Everywhere life expectancy is lengthening. Medicine and surgery improve continually and the perfectly human weakness of the desire to delay death for as long as possible preoccupies all developed societies. This is placing an increasingly intolerable burden on funds. The infirm and old are expensive. They also consume and do not produce, at least for an ever-lengthening amount of their life span.

All our expectations in the early and halcyon days of the welfare state are exploded by these processes. David Lloyd-George introduced the state pension in the UK in 1908. At the time, the number qualifying to draw this benefit was 500,000. Now with the age for retirement having stayed the same, the number is over 12 million. This is about 40% of the total of the population in work. When Nye Bevan introduced the National Health Service (NHS) in the late 1940s in the UK, he confidently forecast that it would improve the nation's health quickly and fade away after a few years: thus are socialist fantasies sold to the public.

These issues are not just affecting developed countries, although they are acute there. Some developing countries have rapidly growing populations which provide an expanding work force to create a tax and income base to assuage these challenges, Nigeria for example. In China, however, the problem is becoming acute because of the communist party's one child per family policy. China has an ageing and declining population which is the single biggest reason for its urgent industrialisation. China is in a desperate race against time. This issue, and the demands it makes on state funds, makes inevitable the decline of state subsidy to enterprises, including steel.

Only economic growth can provide the resources for the private sector or governments to meet these challenges. The dramatic nature of the requirement is demonstrated by consideration of the rate of growth needed in the UK. In order to meet the health, social security and social care needs of the ageing population, plus provide for a real rate of increase in the standard of living for the whole population of only 1% per year, the UK economy must grow at above 3% for the foreseeable future. Only in one decade has the economy grown at that rate: in the 1830s at the height of the industrial revolution. This reality has yet to dawn on our political and administrative elites – it may only do so under popular pressure.

The populism of wealth

The most powerful justification for the assumption that economic growth is a predominant ambition is the behaviour of human beings. Economically advanced and expensive ways of living are popular.

It is understandable that this dominance should have accelerated over the last 20 years. It was only in 1979 that Maoist doctrine was displaced by Deng's reforms and China began the journey to its own economic revival and version of capitalism. India followed with the first wave of financial reforms in the early 1990s. The shift can be seen now as a consequence of the triumph of capitalism in achieving economic recovery after World War II compared to the economic destructiveness of socialism and its decline in its various forms. At the time, this was less obvious; even in the late 1980s the CIA was advising Reagan of the economic dominance of the Soviet Union and its relative success compared to the USA: yet another example of self-interest triumphing over reality. After all, the CIA's existence was threatened if it did not have a powerful opponent to justify its budgets and staffing.

But the dominant factor – and the one which has driven this timing – has been technology. The mobile phone, television and now the internet allow even very poor Chinese, Indian and African villagers to see the living standards of the developed world and to communicate with those who benefit from these standards. What these people see, they want – and politicians will facilitate them achieving their wants or perish in the defence of the old and ineffective. It is so simple. This will not change until living standards are equalised upwards across the globe. It is then possible that we humans will find something else to motivate us – but not until then. Keynes, quoted in the prologue, foresaw this change in ambitions in 1931, but only after another century of economic growth.

This raising of living standards will be achieved in this century unless we experience some sort of catastrophe. During the last century we avoided catastrophes although at the time some events looked like they could become so. Thus, we had the two World Wars, the Depression, communism and the Cold War and the arrival of nuclear weapons. Anthropogenic Global Warming (AGW) is now presented as the next potential catastrophe. Is this the great new threat or just another attempt to dethrone secularism and economic ambition with something more transcendental and religious? It is certainly used by many as a basis for attempted persuasion.

Does AGW dethrone economic growth?

We are assured by some that the abandonment of the pursuit of growth and a return to a more "sustainable", less resource-intensive lifestyle, will be the only adequate response to the supposed threat. The threat is based on climate change forecasts which predict rising temperatures due to human-derived generation of greenhouse gases: beware Warren Buffett's comment about forecasts and forecasters.

There is a long history of dire forecasts of the detrimental impact of human behaviour on the sustainability of life on the planet. These go together with strident exhortations to change our behaviour to something more sustainable. The most famous of these was the doom-laden prediction of Thomas Malthus. The latest, before AGW, and now largely forgotten, being the Club of Rome and its bible, The Limits to Growth. This arose in the mid-1970s following the first oil crisis of 1973. Suddenly there was a mass anxiety about the world running out of oil and there being no adequate alternative. This physical limitation was seen by the Club as placing a ceiling on the possibility for growth. Thus we needed to adapt by developing strategies for a zero-growth world. Nothing of the sort happened, neither the prediction nor the consequence nor the favoured response: in the case of oil and gas the world has about 30 years' reserves at expected consumption levels –the same as it had 40 years ago. This is because of the inherent nature of reserves. They are economically defined. It is not worth establishing reserves through expensive exploration activity beyond 30 years. Meanwhile, extraction techniques improve, extending the life of current wells and bringing feasible extraction to discounted resources. The latest example of this sort is the shale gas phenomenon.

The case of AGW, even if it were to be proven by events, I regard as irrelevant except from a political perspective. There is no way we can deal with this threat except by technological change. The same is true of any other hypothesised threat: global warming believers need not feel singled out for criticism. The seeking of some sea change in human behaviour though exhortation, education or political dictation is unproductive and unachievable. Until the world's population has achieved high living standards they will not listen and they will be correct. Our elites in the West may wish this otherwise; but they are simply self-destructing. Our only answer to this hypothesised threat is through technology and this requires wealth to achieve it, and the faster we grow the easier and sooner technological solutions will be found if they are required.

There is one forecast which is more reliable than any other and that is the one about an ageing population. We know the age structure of the population. We know their life expectancy. Short of some plague on a virulent scale, these trends will play out as I have described. We need economic growth to meet the challenge. If we do not, then we really could face a catastrophe of social, political and generational strife of untold dimensions.

The worst thing to do is what we in the West are now doing. We are adopting a series of measures which are detrimental to the well-being of our populations, suppress economic growth and are counterproductive if the AGW threat exists. We subsidise alternative energy technologies; we impose punitive carbon taxes where no viable technologies exist to be stimulated by these costs; and we exhort our populations at home and abroad to avoid emulating those who are doing the exhortation. Our elites are seeking to pull up the drawbridge to economic well-being behind them, a pernicious objective with the awful potential to create social and political strife.

Subsidies for anything are only there to divert capital from more productive to less productive investment. If the latter were not less productive, it would not need subsidies. The subsidy is designed to raise the return on capital of the affected industry against alternatives – so channelling the investment capital to lower true returns. Subsidies are always only temporary due to this characteristic; counter forces develop, eventually winning the day, especially from those sectors of the economy unfairly penalised by the diversion of capital and from the ultimate payers of the subsidies – the taxpayer. The regular outbreak of policies to provide subsidies is ineradicable; they provide politicians with something to do and something to manipulate. Those who are in receipt of them gain so much that they will corrupt the public debate and political process endlessly to obtain them. There is also the moral glow of doing something to "save the planet". Wherever the few stand to gain at the expense of the many, truth is in jeopardy. It is in double jeopardy when self-interest combines with self-righteousness as is the case for the renewable energy lobby.

Finally, subsidy is inherently backward-looking; it builds a constituency against technological change and adaptation by supporting an established answer to problems. It motivates to pursue the subsidy rather than technology improvement. Technological change is our only available answer to any problem in the world of practical affairs.

So if AGW is not happening, we should push on with economic growth as always; if it is happening, we need to push on even harder. Not a comfortable position to accept for those with their self-interest tied into the hypothesis: all those who receive subsidies or benefit in some way from those that do, and all the academics studying the global warming phenomena. But then, academics are the most conservative of all groups when it comes to any intellectual debate when it affects their careers.

In this debate about the virtues of economic growth, the structure of the population and its consequences must trump all other considerations. We are humans and are only here to benefit from our circumstances. Environmental concerns are relevant only in this context. I feel confident that we do not need to "save the planet", as it will be here long after we are gone and is capable of adapting and taking care of itself better than we are.

Technology: The incredible adaptation machine

I have mentioned above that technological change is our only means of solving any problem. It is the bedrock of all economic growth and human adaptation. Genetic mutation, which is the only means available to other species, is too slow for us. We have, therefore, created and embraced technology. Even as hunter-gatherers, we had some technological development; we developed the use of primitive hand tools to assist in killing and butchering. Planting seeds to grow crops, and the consequential selection of better strains of seeds for further planting, was a technological achievement in itself. Technology is, surely, defined as the use of tools or ideas to intervene in nature to change outcomes to ones perceived to be more desirable.

The dawn of the agrarian revolution was the moment when we sealed the deal between humans and nature and since then we have been committed to using technology to sustain and enhance life and – crucially – to solve whatever problems it brings with it. This is an irrevocable deal. To believe we can adapt any other way - for example through some fundamental change in human behaviour - is to embrace a fantasy, at least until the human desire of the poorer populations for a massively enhanced lifestyle is satisfied.

It took millennia for technological change to interact with economics and create the Industrial Revolution. Security of ownership of assets had been a precondition for the success of the agrarian revolution but for a long time intellectual property was not recognised as an asset in the same way as land, equipment or tools. Someone who invented a new process for making things could not benefit from it except for a short time directly through his own use. An invention could be copied by anyone and used without economic benefit to the inventor. Something truly fundamental occurred in 17th century United Kingdom. The ownership of Intellectual property was recognised in the introduction of private patent law. This is the reason for the Industrial Revolution occurring first in the UK. Inventors came to the UK from the continent in many numbers and indigenous innovation was encouraged. Economic self-interest worked its invisible hand. Patent law was not introduced in continental Europe until the 19th century.

The intellectual capacity for technological change is expanding at a rate which can only be subject to speculation; but it is considerably faster than in any other era. The rate is a function of the brains dedicated to this activity and their interconnectivity: their ability to communicate at speed and share ideas. The number of brains is a function of education and hence is derived from economic wealth and the desire for that result.

Major scientific breakthroughs, The Theory of Relativity, for instance, can result from the genius of individuals, but technological change is most certainly not simply a result of individual genius – it is an intensely social process in which the speed of information exchange is also critical. We are at a stage where the rate of potential technology change is expanding exponentially. The internet with its cheap and universal access combines with expanding research budgets and massive increases in trained personnel to create a reaction rather like a nuclear reaction when it reaches criticality: we are not able to control the result. One measure of the scale of human energy available for such change is that China has as many people studying engineering at university level as there are in the total pool of trained engineers in the UK.

Hence, at this early stage of the 21st century, we are looking to a future of unknowable technical creativity and change. When we look back at the 20th century, we can see that we experienced massive changes of this kind. When Sir Edward Grey, the British Foreign Secretary in 1914, looked out of his office window as dusk gathered on the day he had told the House of Commons that England's declaration of war on Germany was inevitable, he saw a man lighting the gas lamps in St James' Park and memorably said, "The lamps are going out all over Europe. We shall not see them lit again in our lifetime". Note that these were gas lamps. In 1914 we were only at the start of electricity use. At that time we had no idea of television, mobile phones, jet engines, nuclear power, antibiotics, computers, the internet, the shipping container, the contraceptive pill and a thousand other innovations which have revolutionised our lives.

It is almost exactly 100 years since Sir Edward Grey spoke those words; it is inevitably a truism to say that we have little if any idea what innovations will revolutionise our lives over this century. All we know is that they will and will do so immeasurably more than in the last 100 years. These changes will support our need for, and ambition to have, further economic growth; and they will provide the means to solve any problem, environmental or otherwise. If they don't, there is no other solution available – and so we must hope they do that job. When they fail to do it, we may see the extinction of the human race, which, if Darwinian evolution theory is correct, will come about one day when our ecological niche closes around us. Then the forecasters of doom will be proved correct; although I am unsure what value their forecasts will have.

Economic growth in the 21st century

It is the establishment of economics as a subject with a theoretical basis of its own which has facilitated wealth creation through the last two centuries. This is not surprising as economics is the study of wealth creation. The scale of this is easy to underestimate. As a reader of this monograph please pause a moment and estimate how many times the GDP of the globe expanded during the 20th century. Take the time to pour yourself a glass of whisky, or burgundy if that is your taste as it is mine, or make a cup of tea or coffee and perhaps stare out of the window like the overly pessimistic Sir Edward Grey. Take a walk round the block or read the sports section of the paper. Switch your mind from this question and then return to it as the answer is normally a surprise.

If you estimated 27 times you were spot on, or as spot on as the best analysts. In rough terms, that means that in 1900 world GDP was $2 trillion and at the end of the period it was $50 trillion. These numbers are in real terms, eliminating inflation. Most people vastly underestimate this growth and some even estimate that it declined. We did have a number of crises whose impacts are held to have been much more substantial in suppressing growth than they were in reality. There were two World Wars, the twin curses of communism and fascism, the inevitable chaos and discontinuity consequent on the dissolution of several empires, plus a depression and several recessions. Looking at those facts it seems easy to make an underestimate. Yet the facts are there. The spread of education, the host of innovations highlighted before, the desire of people for a better life and the need for governments to respond with at least partially supportive policies, are the reasons for the growth. Underpinning these is the tyranny of compound numbers. After all, an increase of 27 times is only a 3.4 % p.a. growth rate compounded.

The growth rate for economies emerging out of poverty has been increasing; it appears that countries have learnt how to grow and that this has increased the speed of their growth: they have learnt how to grow the rate of growth. It is estimated that for millennia growth rates were much less than 1% p.a. , certainly they were minimal and indeed in past millennia growth did decline at times. Until the dawn of the Industrial Revolution in the UK around the mid-18th century, growth was minimal. Then things began to change. Even then growth rates were not extreme. The fastest decade of growth for the UK was the 1830s, when the rate exceeded 3% p.a. in each year. Something very interesting has happened, for as growth has spread, the rate of growth has increased: for the USA and Germany the fastest decade was at better than 5%, while for Japan it was better than 7% and for China it has been 10%. What accounts for this is policy sophistication as governments and individuals learn from the past, and the fact that the early stages of economic development are about mimicking. Emerging countries copy the industry and technologies of the developed ones and these options are available, well understood and relatively easy to implement.

The great growth of the 20th century involved only a small part of the planet. The economically developed part of the world today constitutes only about 25%, at most, of the population. Western Europe, North America, Japan and a few smaller areas such as South Korea, Singapore, Australia and Taiwan can be regarded as developed, plus minorities in the populations of other countries who enjoy a Western standard of living. There are still over five billion people who aspire to those standards of life. If the world cannot satisfy their desires in a generation or at most two, hence by the second half of this century, we must expect political and military turmoil on an unprecedented scale, as their resentment at their conditions builds to a point of geo-political and military action.

Of human freedom

Humans have evolved a desire for freedom. Freedom is not a qualitative but a quantitative condition: people can have more or less of it. The desire seems to be well established. This is clear over the last 200 years. It is also one of the requirements for technological innovation and hence for economic growth. Without freedom no innovation would be possible as innovation requires liberty of thought and the free exchange of ideas: witness the decline into stasis of communist Russia and its satellites. Without innovation no economic growth is possible. This is a fundamental challenge for China.

But the search for freedom is not a given, as the state of freedom brings stress as it requires individuals to take responsibility for their actions and so make choices. It is the enemy of sloth and inaction, indeed it is the enemy of contentment, yet it seems to be a universal desire. The desire is frustrated for periods and seems in retreat for periods. The stress it causes can lead to the search for the security of subservience and escape from individual responsibility to totalitarianism in the face of perceived external threats. But, freedom leads to growth and growth enhances the capacity for freedom. Regimes which deny freedom perish, such as the Soviet Union. We must hope for the continuation of this virtuous circle.

More than that, its existence is one of the conditions without which nothing is capable of being forecast, or envisioned.

The ferrous world

The next three chapters will look at the future of steel and the ferrous world in general. My envisaging will be built on the preconceptions and beliefs articulated above. I am an optimist whose optimism is tempered by the belief that nothing is continuous and so periods when freedom recedes, or growth is lost are to be expected even if they cannot be predicted. Given the centrality of steel to economic growth and civilisation itself and my firm conviction that growth will be forthcoming during this century, the reader will not be surprised that I see the future as holding exciting promise for the steel industry. I hope I have let the reader see a little, in the spirit of Mr Buffett, into the forecaster rather than the forecast. Now I will turn to the forecast.

CHAPTER FIVE

Long run drivers of steel demand

"If you can't convince them; confuse them". Anon. Old consulting motto.

A pessimist or an optimist?

As the chapter on forecasting in general demonstrated, I am an optimist concerning long-term economic growth at least for the balance of this century. However, the future of the total world economy does not imply anything about individual industrial sectors. This chapter will explore the future of steel consumption; and especially whether optimism or pessimism is appropriate for steel.

The world is made up of optimists and pessimists. Sometimes we are both, depending on different circumstances and different times. Timing can be everything, and when combined with a long view of history, is a sure basis for success in economic matters. Keynes was indeed right when he said, "in the long run we are all dead". That did not stop him from taking a considered view of the long run and making a fortune for his Cambridge college, King's, from shrewd investments made in stocks and shares at the nadir of the Great Depression. As we saw in the prologue he was a long term optimist, even though he would be dead.

In 1972 the US steel industry's most respected commentator, Father Hogan of Fordham University, expected US steel consumption to be 250Mt in 10 years, by 1982. It was then 150Mt and never grew much beyond that number. Only 24 months ago, in the winter of 2011/12, some senior executives in the industry were talking of the arrival of "Peak Steel". The idea of Peak Steel seems to be that somehow there is a ceiling for steel consumption and the current stresses in the global economy will result in that ceiling being reached now or in the near future. This opinion was articulated in particular by the chairman of the then Nippon Steel. Even The Financial Times printed stories with this in its headline. I find the idea to be little more than an expression of despair brought on by the sudden change in expectations following the global financial crisis – which was in reality only a North Atlantic crisis. It is the blinkered view of someone unable to view the long term because of the strain and stress of coping with the immediate crisis: not an unusual phenomenon. That is not a good basis for forecasting – which we must now attempt for steel demand and supply. The industry and its observers and commentators do not have a glorious past when it comes to accuracy in forecasting.

There is a strong tendency, as illustrated above, for the industry to be beset by excessive pessimism or optimism. The US industry is a good example of this volatility of view. In the early 1970s excessive optimism ruled, witness Father Hogan - an esteemed historian of the US steel industry. Then global demand was expanding at 6% p.a., and had done since 1947. US demand, illustrated in Exhibit 5.1, was at about 150Mtp.a.

In the event, US growth did plateau and, with the growth of imports, local producers were heavily loss-making by 1984. The pessimism that broke out in the late 1970s was so deep that it coloured all thought of the future. US producers, and others in the developed economies, grossly misread the emergence of Chinese demand.

The Chinese development - minorities are sometimes right

In 1995 the American Iron and Steel Institute (AISI), whose members at the time included all the blast furnace based integrated steel producers in the US and Canada, invited me and another outside commentator to attend their annual conference in West Virginia. I was asked to give my opinion on what the level of world demand, for crude steel, would be by 2010, 15 years hence. At the time crude steel demand was growing at about 1% p.a., it had been at that level or thereabouts for the last 20 years. Total demand was about 750Mt. I predicted a figure of 1.1 - 1.2 billion tonnes p.a. by 2010. The audience was uncomprehending. How could this number be serious when we were at 750Mt? There was only one reason, but it was in my mind incontrovertible: China.

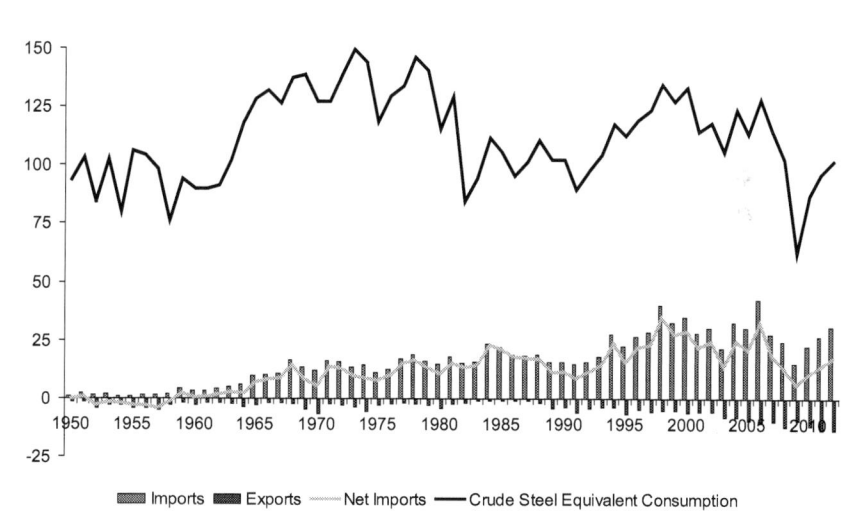

EXHIBIT 5.1: US STEEL CONSUMPTION WITH NET IMPORTS /Mt

■ Imports ■ Exports —— Net Imports —— Crude Steel Equivalent Consumption

Source: worldsteel, AISI and Hatch

I argued that China was on a path of urbanisation and industrialisation which was almost inevitably going to be achieved in the absence of some internal political catastrophe on the scale of Maoism. This path was well established, having commenced in 1979. It had already resulted in steel growth from less than 20Mt p.a. to about 100Mt and the future of the communist party depended on providing enhanced living standards for its population. The scale of this development was as never before seen on the planet and any preconceptions held in the West would be inapplicable. It was also going to be very steel intensive as it would have to be focused on infrastructure and manufacturing given the backward nature of the country and the mass of people to be employed. I estimated Chinese steel production and consumption at 500Mt by 2010. I pointed out that this fivefold increase was only the same as the scale of growth between 1980 and the meeting we were attending. In the event, I was conservative. It was approximately 600Mt.

Nobody in the audience believed me. A plethora of objections were raised and felt to be conclusive: after all China was communist and the Soviet empire had just collapsed – that demonstrated how unsustainable communist economic ambitions were. Wherever was China going to get the capital from to invest in this capacity? What about the raw materials? What about the technical skills to build and run such an industry? Whilst my view was respected, I was felt to be a little out of touch with reality. I have never been invited back to give my views on other topics. Being an optimist, I am still hopeful.

There are follies of hindsight as well as follies of foresight. Chinese steel growth then appeared virtually absurd at least to the leaders of the industry in North America, and they were not alone. It is wise to take account of the wider social, human and cultural context of economic activity, as I have argued in the previous chapter, and not to take accepted wisdom on trust. Indeed, it is my view that whenever there is an overwhelming consensus around anything of an economic or social nature, the right opinion turns out to be different. By the time the consensus is established and "it is obviously right", reality has moved on and the view has become time-expired. We might usefully ask ourselves to what does this judgement apply in current consensus thinking?

Irrationality about the long-term prospects for steel is accountable at least partially by the volatility of short-term prospects but this is reinforced by managerial turnover. It is seldom the case, except in family-controlled businesses, that senior managers stay in post for longer than five years. In an industry with regular and dramatic changes of circumstances this is unfortunate – leaders need time to learn and develop judgment which requires at least two cycles for it to be acquired. Of course, long tenure can lead to ossification of view and loss of learning capacity; managerial policy is another area of judgment rather than science. Expectations are regularly, and often suddenly, not met. These then lead to periods of extreme financial stress and distress. In these circumstances, it is understandable that industry leaders experience uncertainty about the future; and humans often deal with uncertainly by becoming unduly pessimistic.

The long run

In thinking long term, I have three time periods in mind, although not rigidly. These relate to the perspectives which are suited to different decisions and decision-makers. Five years is the period that operational plans should use as their focus. Obviously 12 months is the period for budgetary planning but if significant changes are planned then five years is the normal perspective. Fifteen years is the normal period for strategic planning – although with differing degrees of detail for the earlier and later times. The core of the iron and steelmaking process is the hot end: the coke ovens, blast furnaces and basic oxygen vessels or, alternatively, EAFs. This hot and liquid phase is the most capital-intensive and therefore needs the longest planning horizon of any steelmaking and processing assets. Blast furnaces are relined at intervals of 15 – 20 years, so it is economically dangerous to do this without a clear view as to their utility over that period.

In addition, it is necessary to have a 50 year view of likely developments. If you are an iron ore miner -and that includes many steel companies as 30% of all iron ore is supplied through captive mines - then you do, or should, plan 50 years ahead. It takes at least 10 years to plan a mine and bring it into production, from establishing the reserves and resources, through drilling and testing, to financing and building the mine and infrastructure, and then shipping the first product. This is the timescale for a new major mine, not an incremental extension or minor deposit in an established zone with infrastructure in place. The required deposit size for the major miners to justify investment needs to be over 1bn t of delivered product: 50 years at 20Mt p.a. But this is a minimum. Ideally, it should be 2.5 bn: 50Mt p.a. by 50 years, or bigger. This scale provides an optimal size for capital investment in mine and infrastructure and overall scale to justify the large allocation of management overhead to the development program.

It is these new ventures which are required for major volumes to feed current and future steel industry demand. The current new iron ore zones, such as West Africa, require massive investment into infrastructure, railroads and ports especially, but also support services such as power stations and townships due to mines often being in remote locations. Making these commitments requires not just large balance sheets, but a very high level of confidence in long-term plans. There is a current example of a major new iron ore mine under development which is expected to produce 100Mt p.a. of ore, and requires a total of $20-22bn in capital. This includes rail and port as well as mine investment.

So in developing a view of the future, we need to bear these three periods in mind. In this chapter I shall focus on the very long term which is the 50 years or beyond. Later I will review and forecast shorter term developments.

The drivers of long-term demand

It is a first principle of the universe that everything is connected to everything else. What then are the principle drivers of steel consumption? A number of factors are critical but how they should be combined or balanced is not clear. Of obvious importance is population. The fewer the people in the world the less steel is required; and the more people the more steel, other things being equal. However, other things are seldom equal. The amount and nature of the resources those people use is critical and this is related to the level of income they enjoy. But then not all societies are the same in their economic structure: some are very manufacturing-intensive and others less so – even being essentially service-only economies; although these tend to be small such as Singapore.

There is a widely held view that economies have a general tendency to experience a substantial decrease in the ratio of steel to GDP as GDP per person advances beyond a certain stage and service activities become more important. There is then, also, a natural predisposition to apply the declining intensity model to the globe as a whole. It is these two tendencies and predispositions which I will examine in the rest of this chapter.

If there were a direct continuous relation between GDP and steel use then, if the world's GDP grew by the same 27 times in this century as it did in the last, the world would need about 25bn tonnes of steel each year by 2100. Not even the most fanatical steel optimist would support such a hypothesis. That "forecast" looks absurd. So some decline in intensity is to be expected, but what and how much?

Where and for what is steel used?

A place to start is by understanding how and for what purpose steel is used. Globally, construction accounts for about 50% of steel use and this seems to vary only modestly in relation to an economy's maturity.

For example it is 40% in the USA and 60% in China. All economic activity requires construction. In the early stages a society is building railroads, ports, electrical power plants, water-treatment plants, etc. It, also in tandem, builds factories for production of manufactured products. As cities grow, they grow upwards as well as outwards and skyscrapers demand steel for strength. As the economy moves to services, this also requires construction. Roads, with much In the way of steel for bridges, are added to railroads. Air terminals are added to seaports. As food distribution is required for cities, warehousing and distribution facilities as well as shops expand. Construction is required for all forms of economic activity. It might be lighter in weight at different stages of development – a distribution warehouse does not require the same steel as a power plant – but it is still required in large quantities.

EXHIBIT 5.2: REGIONAL STEEL USE BY SECTOR/Mt

2012	Automotive	Equipment	Shipbuilding	Construction	Oil and Gas	Metal goods	Total
China	81	174	28	298	37	66	684
CIS	6	13	2	25	8	5	60
Developed Asia	18	33	7	69	8	16	151
Eastern Europe	4	8	1	14	2	4	33
India	8	15	3	41	3	7	76
MENA	8	21	2	53	6	7	97
North America	17	23	5	44	9	15	113
Oceania	1	2	0	3	1	1	7
Other developing Asia	7	15	2	30	4	7	66
South America	8	16	2	30	5	8	70
Sub Saharan Africa	1	3	0	5	1	1	12
Western Europe	19	34	5	59	7	18	143
Total	180	356	57	672	91	155	1,511

Source: McKinsey

After construction, another 25% of steel goes into a wide range of capital investment: plant for production of goods such as automobiles, domestic appliances, chemical products, and supporting forging and fabrication facilities. All these and many more uses consume large quantities of often high-quality steels. Even the steel industry itself consumes a lot of its own product. In the early 1970s when the British Steel Corporation, under state-ownership, was undergoing modernisation and expansion, it consumed 10% of its own production for a couple of years. Finally, about 25% of steel goes for use in consumer goods, such durables as the automobiles that are assembled, as well as disposables. Here, there are a myriad of common everyday uses we are all familiar with such as tin cans, batteries, and a thousand small items. Even a little bit gets into laptops and other electronic devices, including the computer on which I am writing this sentence. One educated view of steel use by sector and by geography is provided in Exhibit 5.2

Drivers of steel demand: Fixed capital formation

Given the importance of capital investment to steel use it can be argued that the best driver for the forecasting of steel demand is fixed capital formation (FCF), that is, expenditure on infrastructure, construction and capital equipment. These sectors consume about 75% of all steel and this seems quite stable across time and different economies. This seems unlikely to reduce; if anything, it might increase at the expense of other materials such as concrete as the strength characteristics of steel are of particular importance in these sectors. If lighter materials are to grow, it will likely be in more consumer goods-oriented products such as transport and consumer durables. FCF is a remarkably consistent percentage of world GDP. It varies only between 20 and 25% of total GDP. For the decades from 1980 to 2000 it trended downwards as developed economies trended towards consumption and services which are generally regarded as being less capital-intensive than manufacturing. During this period there were no large population centres entering rapid economic development. In addition, the infrastructure required in developed countries was already heavily invested and maintenance, whilst required, uses less steel than new construction. Certainly much infrastructure has a very long life.

Chinese development has changed this trend of decline in FCF and now the figure for FCF is close to 25%, possibly an all-time high. Given the requirement for infrastructure and emphasis on manufacturing in China this is easy to understand. China will mature and is doing so, but India and other countries are emerging with the same drivers as China. Given the 75% of the world's population still awaiting Western living standards requiring industrialisation and urbanisation, the percentage of GDP devoted to FCF is hardly likely to drop much below 24-25% of GDP, except for economic cycles, during the first half of this century.

FCF is highly cyclical, much more so than total GDP. The reason is that capital investment decisions by governments can be delayed without any short-term detrimental impact on living standards, and corporations can conserve cash very quickly and without the stresses of asset rationalisation by reducing capital expenditures. There is also a widespread use by governments of income stabilisers, such as unemployment and other benefits, during recessions, which act to support consumer but not capital expenditures. So for short and medium-term forecasting, FCF seems less reliable than more stable drivers such as GDP. In addition, there is no clear analysis and algorithm for relating FCF to an economy's maturity and there does seem to be a strong correlation between maturity and steel intensity of use and, therefore, demand at least this relationship is generally acknowledged and used. So, in considering long-term demand, we must look at this steel intensity issue.

GDP, population and steel intensity as drivers

There is a model used extensively in forecasting steel use at a national level which relates population and GDP per head to total steel usage. This approach has the benefits of simplicity and ease of understanding and communication. It does sound "reasonable". It is claimed that economies tend to converge on a common profile of evolution. The exceptions, or anomalies, to this profile seem explicable by divergent economic structure. This profile is clearly identifiable in the Exhibit 5.3

EXHIBIT 5.3: CRUDE STEEL CONSUMPTION GROWTH TRAJECTORY FOR SELECTED REGIONS (2012)

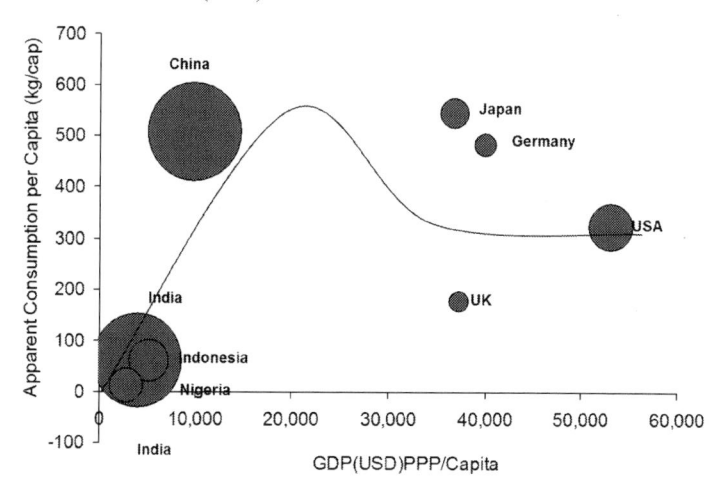

Note: Size of bubble represents population; Source: worldsteel, EIU and Hatch

Individual economies show a strong tendency to a bell-shaped curve of development, but where the declining curve is rather flatter than the ascending one. As GDP grows, so steel intensity, the weight of steel required for each $ of GDP, rises sharply, but after a point, at about $20,000 per person, the weight of steel required per unit of additional GDP declines. This pattern is visible for North America and most of Europe. Outliers from this trend include Japan and Korea and, within

Europe, Germany. But these are all economies which are manufacturing-intensive. They have major manufactured goods balance of payments surpluses and manufacturing constitutes a higher than average percentage of their GDP. Not all countries can do this – global exports must equal global imports and the above-average numbers for these countries must be matched by a downwards effect in other countries. Variations within individual countries would exhibit similar patterns across their regions, such as Florida versus Ohio in the USA.

The declining steel intensity of highly developed countries can be seen as a reciprocal of the very high steel intensity of certain others, namely the manufacturing-intensive economies. China can be viewed as an extreme case. Japan established a model for economic development which included high levels of exported manufactured goods; as a country lacking raw materials, including oil, this was seen as essential to pay for such imports. The USA was a facilitator of this direction, wanting Japan to develop rapidly as a demonstration of the virtues of capitalism in contrast to communist China.

South Korea followed Japan as did Taiwan. These are relatively small countries. China has become an extremely large follower. Under very clear central government direction and facilitated by a high savings rate, the highest in the world at close to 50%, and lack of currency convertibility, China has relied on a very high infrastructure and construction spend plus investment into manufacturing with a strong export bias. Thus it has shifted a major proportion of its population from agrarian subsistence to urbanised relative affluence in 20 years.

The FCF element of China's economy is distorted upwards from the mean with the result that it utilises about 500kg of steel per head of population whilst only having a GDP per head, even at purchasing power parity, of $10k. These reported numbers are overly simplistic and must be adjusted in myriad ways if we are to see the underlying steel requirements of an economy.

An observation is not an explanation – and it is not immediately clear what causes declining steel intensity; furthermore, on closer scrutiny, an observed pattern might hide more subtle and detailed contrasting patterns. This is indeed true when we look more closely at steel intensity. A simple pattern turns out to be very complex.

Adjusting for steel yield

The first adjustment, and the simplest, is to take account of yield between crude and finished steel. The efficiency of an industry between crude steel and finished use can vary greatly between countries and over time within a country. In China, for example, there are hundreds of steel producers - many have outdated and small-scale assets. The assets are often fragmented involving high levels of intermediate inventories. These inventories result in increased movement of product, which always adds cost but also results in some yield loss through damage etc. The result is lower levels of productivity between liquid steel and usable finished steel such as hot dipped galvanised (HDG) for automotive assembly or structural steel work for high rise buildings. In addition not all use of steel is efficient to the standards of the fully developed world. How much finished steel is actually currently required by China is impossible to measure but I would assert that perhaps the crude numbers are 20% inflated by the inefficiencies in the value chain. Thus, the 500kg per head might be 400kg in ex-mill finished steel requirement if the industry was run to the standards of a Western economy.

This understanding of finished steel use from crude steel production applies to understanding developed world steel figures. Exhibit 1.3 illustrates this perfectly. It is only finished steel which matters and supports a quality of life which is reflected in GDP. The chart here shows numbers for steel production and yield changes for the German steel industry. In crude steel terms, the country consumes as much now as it did 30 years ago. It appears thus to have declined in intensity as its GDP is much greater. But in finished steel terms, the economy of

Germany utilises much more steel now than it did 30 years ago. It is finished steel that is used, not crude steel. This is because yields have improved by about 30%. This pattern of improvement is mimicked in all developed economies over this time. Thus, a large part of the apparent decline in intensity associated in analysts' minds with the shift of developed economies towards services is illusionary. What they are seeing is changes in the efficiency of the industry itself. The decline is only in crude steel intensity and this is because the steel industry has massively improved its efficiency through technologies such as continuous casting. What about the future? These yield improvements will continue but at a declining rate. The big gains from such developments are now taken. Future increases in steel use will more clearly require increases in crude steel production.

Adjusting for trade in steel-containing products

There are further limitations to the intensity curve; some acknowledged and some not. The manufacturing-intensive countries export steel in the form of goods - "hidden" steel exports - whilst the other countries import those goods - "hidden" steel imports. The curve of declining steel intensity at high income levels needs to be adjusted for this factor. The cars imported to a country are consumed there and constitute local steel use, just as are locally produced cars. The local intensity of finished steel consumption can and should be adjusted for this trade. In global terms it makes no difference to a forecast as there is a balancing of effects, but it does make a large difference to local numbers.

Worldsteel publishes numbers for apparent and true steel use (TSU) per capita. The numbers for the major economies for 2011 are in Exhibit 5.4. This clearly illustrates the distortion effects of not adjusting for steel used in traded manufactured goods. Japan has a true steel use number less than the USA by about 40kg per person, whilst having an apparent steel use of approximately 200kg more. Again, Germany, because of its positive trade balance in manufactured, steel-intensive goods has a true steel use about 80kg per person less than its apparent use. In the case of Korea the anomaly is nearly 400kg. Thus, true steel use in this sense of allocating trade in finished goods is recognised, and can be accounted for to some degree of accuracy.

EXHIBIT 5.4: APPARENT AND TRUE FINISHED STEEL CONSUMPTION PER CAPITA (kg/capita)

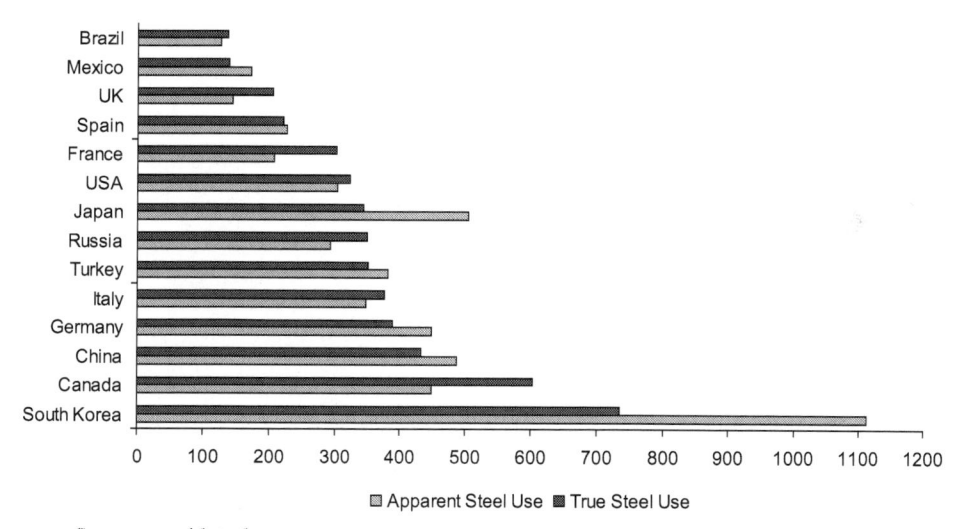

Source: worldsteel

Unacknowledged allocations of steel use

There are further distortions which are not dealt with in Worldsteel numbers or elsewhere, in my experience. Traded steel-containing goods require capital investment in plant and machinery and in infrastructure and transport to move those goods to their point of use in another country. These investments contain much steel. What is the correct way of dealing with the steel which is this capital stock? The only difference between the products and the fixed assets is that the products are physically relocated before their use. If they were miraculously to be made in the using country in the future, then the capital stock required, and the steel used therein, would be accounted part of that country.

Indeed, this happened in the 1980s when Japanese automotive manufacturers relocated capacity to the USA to avoid trade friction and secure their market share. According to the logic above, the steel used in building and equipping those plants would have been accounted for, whether imported or made locally, as part of the US steel-intensity calculation. It follows then that the steel in the plants in Japan making the cars for the US market before relocation of production should be accounted for as part of US steel intensity.

There are two important theoretical points here. When we talk about steel intensity for an economy we are surely talking about the amount of steel required by that political-economic entity to support the way of life which it enjoys. In the case of the USA it is that country's way of life which is supported by Japanese car exports in the 1970s and 80s and now by Chinese exports of a range of goods. This observation is reinforced by the fact that it is US incomes which buy those products. They constitute part of the US consumer's expenditure. This is one reason why the physical location of the production should play no part in any calculation of country specific steel intensity.

In steel discussions about the future the steel intensity curve is used extensively. It is used to show that as economies mature and they become more focused on services rather than manufacturing the steel required for each unit of GDP reduces. But this reduction is not what it seems. The amount of steel required to support these service-intensive economies is much higher than anyone is thinking. What we see is only the result of international specialisation and comparative advantage.

The second theoretical reason pertains to the specific purpose which I am pursuing; which is to understand the long-run steel intensity of the world, not any individual country. In this context, again, the location of production is immaterial. It would be quite incorrect to conclude that as the world economy progresses and it becomes, in total, more service-intensive over time, then it will become as little steel-intensive as the USA and, say, the UK seem to have become. Yet, this is exactly the kind of inference which is being drawn in discussions about the long-term demand for steel. If and when the global economy develops so that all countries have a high GDP and are service-intensive, they will still need goods as the USA does today. The USA, for example, will still import or, perhaps more likely, will revert to manufacturing these goods for itself as labour rates and other costs equalise across the globe.

As about 25% of steel use is in fixed capital assets other than infrastructure and construction, then this is not a trivial subject, although I do not know how to account with accurate mathematics for this. For a simplistic example, we can look at South Korea. It has an apparent steel use of nearly 1,200 kg per person. Its Worldsteel "true steel use" is near to 725kg. Thus 450kg is net exports. At 25% of steel use, about 180kg goes to fixed assets for manufacturing and most of this is for exports of steel-intensive goods. Maybe, then, South Korea's "true steel use" number needs to be reduced by a further 100kg per person, taking it to 625kg per person.

A last – but major - adjustment

There is another adjustment which is required but which is not generally acknowledged. Transport is required to take steel-containing products to their country of consumption. Cargo requires ships to transport it, so manufactured goods going from China to the US and Europe use container ships. Oil going from the Persian Gulf to the same destinations likewise requires Cape-size bulk vessels. These vessels are steel-intensive but the steel to make them is recorded as steel consumption in the country of construction. So, today China is the world's biggest shipbuilder. In addition to ships to conduct trade, there has to be a major development in infrastructure. Ports, rail lines etc. are required for import but also for export of product. Shipbuilding and related infrastructure,, for exported goods, I would assess, represents 7.5% of all steel use - about 112Mt in 2013. In Exhibit 5.2 shipbuilding alone is 4% of steel use and this excludes equipment such as engines etc. for the ships.

The country of consumption for this material is, in fact, the country which uses the ships to supply its product: the use is in support of that country's economic well-being. This is identical in principle to the points about the manufacturing plant investment. The US has virtually no shipbuilding industry, except for military vessels, yet its economy is approximately 22% of global GDP. Other things being equal, it should, therefore, be allocated 22% of the steel used in ship construction and related infrastructure to support exports to the USA. This is 25Mt of steel p.a. This is about 75kg per head for the population of 330 million. I will cease further calculation for the purpose of this analysis. Here, it is the principle which is important.

Now let us estimate the fully adjusted "true steel use" of the USA. According to worldsteel, apparent steel use in 2012 was 308kg per head of population. Net indirect imports were 12.4Mt. This is approximately 38kg per person. If each tonne of indirect steel imported requires a third of a tonne of fixed assets to produce it, then we should add a further 13kg. But if we now add the shipping required, then we add another 75kg. Thus, the adjusted TSU figure is 308 + 38 + 13 + 75: a total of 444kg per person. This is nearly 50% greater than the apparent steel consumption figure and nearly 25% higher than the worldsteel "true steel use" number. Interestingly it is a steel intensity which is almost the same as the apparent intensity number in China.

The steel intensity curve is used and misused

The steel intensity curve is used in discussion to argue that steel intensity declines with higher GDP per head, and thus that at maturity, there will be a levelling-off of growth, and a peak of steel use will be reached; there might even be a decline. Whilst a curve of this nature is indisputable, it is seriously misused as it is poorly understood. The decline of steel intensity is much less than the apparent decline and much less than generally understood. Manufacturing-intensive economies such as China and South Korea are much less steel-intensive than they appear. Less steel-intensive countries such as the USA are much more intensive than they appear. There is no reason to believe that as the global economy matures and development equalises, then steel use will rapidly decline for each unit of added GDP. Yes, there will be a decline, but it will be much less than current thinking suggests. The error here is both in the maths of the curve and in the application of a country model to the global economy as a whole.

Most importantly, what the adjustments discussed tell us is that whilst there is a decline in steel intensity, it is an invalid assumption to expect the pattern of intensity in the emerging economies to replicate the apparent curve of the developed economies. Given that the adjusted true steel use is much higher than the "true steel use" of worldsteel, the level at which Peak Steel might emerge is much higher than anyone expects. Today, the steel intensity of the emerging economies is much lower than apparent reporting indicates, and that of the developed economies much higher.

What the curve does tell us is that international economic comparative advantage changes over time as economies go through different stages of maturity. This should surprise no one. Thus the UK, then the USA, then Germany and Japan to some extent, were leaders in steel-intensive manufacturing. Now South Korea and China take up this role. Soon others will follow and the order will change again. Comparative advantage is not stable. The cost of local raw materials, energy and labour change over time and they change relatively between nations and regions. Today with the arrival of shale gas, the USA manufacturing and energy sectors are experiencing a recovery in their comparative advantage. Steel-intensive manufacturing will recover in the USA and the apparent steel consumption will recover. The adjusted TSU, however, will stay the same. It will also grow over time but probably at a decreasing rate.

My analysis condemns the concept of Peak Steel to "Alice in Wonderland". Reallocating steel consumption between countries is of great interest: it demonstrates the opportunity for steel manufacturing when comparative advantage changes, as it is now, in favour of North America. However, analysing and incorporating trade in various ways does not alter global steel figures. It should inform a better understanding of local country-specific futures but not the future for the planet as a whole.

This simplifies the task of looking to the future as we can use global numbers and take, as the keys to forecasting, GDP and population alone. As argued in earlier chapters, we only need to assume continuing economic growth to be able to derive reasonable estimates of steel requirements, assuming for now no other limitations such as raw material availability and negative material substitution.

Basic assumptions (with thanks to the UN)

So population and GDP are the starting points. The world's population in 2050 is well modelled by the UN. The population in 2010 was some 6.9bn people. By 2050 the UN prediction is for a high of 10.9bn, a low of 8.3bn and a median, or most likely, of 9.6bn. The best estimates suggest a population of 11bn by 2100, although this number is more speculative and requires a pattern of smaller families to be prevalent in all countries as they mature. The population numbers are driven by demographics, particularly family size. This is very culturally dependent, however, hence the range of predicted outcomes. I will take the median as the starting assumption for 2050 and 11bn as the long-term number for the planet. GDP forecasts are also made by the UN and these are in the table at Exhibit 5.5 which also provides the basic numbers for population, GDP per head and steel demand. These numbers are driven by consensus growth forecasts but largely depend on the macro and cultural assumptions made in previous chapters. Exhibit 5.5 provides a neat summary of UN forecasts.

EXHIBIT 5.5: WORLD POPULATION, GDP AND STEEL CONSUMPTION 2010 AND 2050

	2010	2050
Total Population – World		
Low Fertility/bn	6.9	8.3
Medium Fertility/bn	6.9	9.6
High Fertility/bn	6.9	10.9
GPD at PPP* – World/USD bn	75,539	280,613
GDP Per Capita - World		
Low Fertility/USD	10,922.1	33,639.7
Medium Fertility/USD	10,922.1	29,380.6
High Fertility/USD	10,922.1	25,819.0
Steel Consumption Per Capita Forecast		
Low Fertility/kg crude steel	228.6	388.1
Medium Fertility/kg crude steel	228.6	378.7
High Fertility /kg crude steel	228.6	367.7
Total Steel Consumption Forecast		
Low Fertility/bn t crude steel	1.6	3.2
Medium Fertility/bn t crude steel	1.6	3.6
High Fertility/bn t crude steel	1.6	4.0

*PPP: Purchasing Power Parity; Source: worldsteel, PWC, UN, IMF and Hatch

World per capita crude steel consumption is 228.6kg (2010). In the developed world it is approximately 350kg, but country-specific numbers as widely understood need very substantial adjustment to be usable for the world as a whole as it matures economically. This developed-world number needs to be adjusted as discussed above. I propose to use the USA as the model for long-term developed-economy steel usage. For the longest-term assumption which corresponds to a world whose economy is largely mature and growing at the averaged pace of the EU or USA today and from a similar GDP per head as the USA, I will use my fully adjusted true steel use today for the USA. I have allowed for some modest growth from today over the coming decades to get to a per head number for a fully mature economy of 500kg. So it is easy to draw a first approximation of what world steel consumption will be when the world's population is living in a state of economic development involving a genuine steel maturity; which I take as happening sometime between 2050 and 2100, depending on the country.

EXHBIT 5.6: LOG BASE 2 GLOBAL ACCUMULATED ANNUAL STEEL PRODUCTION/Mt

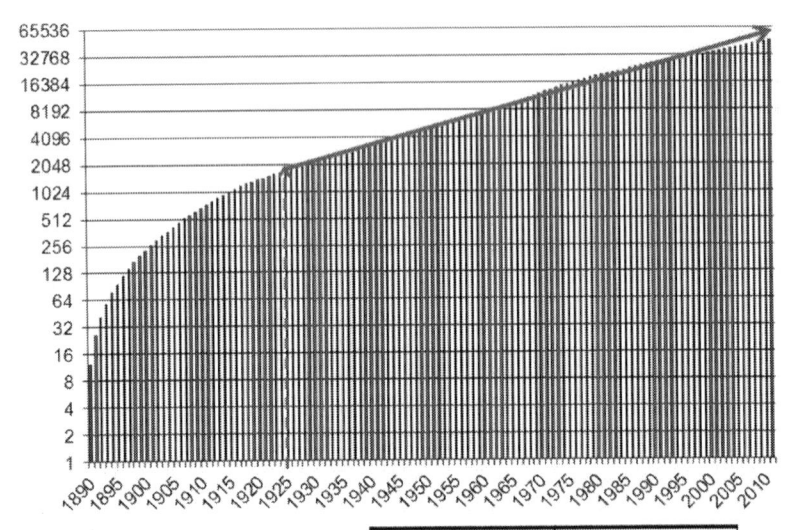

Elapsed Periods for Total Steel production to Double since 1928

Period	Number of Years
1928 - 1945	17
1945 - 1962	17
1962 - 1976	14
1976 - 1998	21
1998 – 2023 (est. on linear basis)	25

Source: IISI/worldsteel, Zimmerman, Hogan, AISI, JISF and Hatch

The summary numbers for crude steel demand, in tonnes, are 3.6bn in 2050 and 5.5bn in 2100. The 2050 number reflects my assessment of steel demand per person. I have taken this as equivalent to that in the developed economies today. By 2050 the average GDP per head is forecast to be around $25,000; which cuts the steel intensity chart at about 320-340 kg per person. This generates the total steel demand I am estimating. As these numbers are based on a 2010 year which was a low year, although maybe not a nadir, they need to be brought to an average. I would suggest an increment of 10% is required for this. Thus, a fully adjusted demand forecast for 2050 is 3.96bn tonnes. To generate a capacity forecast it is necessary to consider the requirement for spare capacity as explored in depth previously. On this basis we need to add 15% to predict a capacity requirement; this is 4.55bn. The 2013 demand is expected to be 1.5 bn. Exhibit 5.5 provides a chart of these numbers.

It is interesting to compare this envisioned future with the following Exhibit 5.6. If the current pace of doubling in annual steel production is 25 years as in the Exhibit then by 2050 production will have trebled from today. This is remarkably consistent with my envisaged numbers above.

Charts such as this provide reference points for sanity checking numbers - they do not provide any explanation or provide a reasoned basis for prediction. However, the chart shows that steel production has a remarkable consistency in doubling every 18 - 20 years since 1930. This looks also to be independent of economic or political turbulence. If this pattern was repeated, then by 2030 production would be 3.0bn tonnes; by 2047 it would be 6.0bn. I am expecting this pattern to be broken and steel demand only to double over the next 25 years.

I have addressed at length the "sine qua non" assumptions about the world in a previous chapter. Human aspiration has surprised us in the last 50 years. The expectation for development in China was pessimistic under Mao: what a surprise has been their development over the last 20 years. Likewise India seemed trapped in socialist planning and the heritage of British bureaucracy - the so-called licensing Raj, following independence - but has at least partially slipped those chains following the reforms of the early 1990s. The reason is simple. The human being seeing living standards, health, food, housing, consumer goods and entertainment, as they exist in the West, desires them. Technology has destroyed space and distance and existing conservative expectations.

The village no longer exists as a boundary for experience and ambition. People the world over want what I have writing this, and they will get it!

There is a tyranny in small numbers if they are compounded over long time periods. People's rising ambitions and expectations plus the ability of economies to learn how to grow could well surprise on the upside. Over the 20th century the world's GDP, inflation-adjusted, grew 27 times. This seems incredible but it is only a 3.4% p.a.. Interestingly, this is the IMF's expectation for global growth in 2014. Despite all the tribulations of the century, the world economy prospered. Over the next decade Goldman Sachs bank expects world GDP to grow by 4% p.a. Even in 2013, with all the low to zero growth in the developed world, total GDP will grow by more than 3%. The speed of growth in the emerging world is accelerating – a perspective often hard to appreciate in the sclerotic world of Europe. At this speed the world's GDP will double in 16 years, so by 2100, my maximum planning horizon, GDP will be approximately 32 times as big as in 2013. I am expecting steel demand to be less than 4 times as big as 2013. My forecast might well be very low. During the century when GDP grew 27 times, steel production grew about 40 times.

Why is steel growth so sluggish?

The above discussion about GDP and steel growth begs the question – why will steel demand grow so slowly? How can the world's economies grow so much and steel so little? By 2050 the UN expects world GDP to be nearly four times what it is today, whereas I expect steel demand to be less than three times the current number by 2050. Steel demand growth does taper off as an economy matures – it is just that this is less dramatic than the steel intensity curve believers assume. Exhibit 5.7 is the curve of steel demand against GDP per head which I am using. This does show a slowing rate of growth but it indicates a maturity peak at about 500kg per head at around $60k personal income.

We need to believe in this slowdown of intensity if the world is not going to need even more steel, maybe 10bn or more tonnes p.a. by 2100. But it is not possible, in my mind, to believe in a smaller demand expectation. Most of this increase in demand will occur in the next 40 years as the pace of industrialisation and urbanisation continues and growth spreads from China to India and then to numerous other smaller but ambitious countries.

Shorter time scales will be the subject of envisaging in the next chapter. This is somewhat more urgent for current managers and planners. But the long term should not be forgotten. In the current gloom and almost despair, it is easy to forget the long-term viability of steel as a material and the world's need for this material in unprecedented quantities. Steel is a material and an industry of the future just as much as it has been of the past.

EXHIBIT 5.7: STEEL CONSUMPTION PER CAPITA FORECAST/(kg)

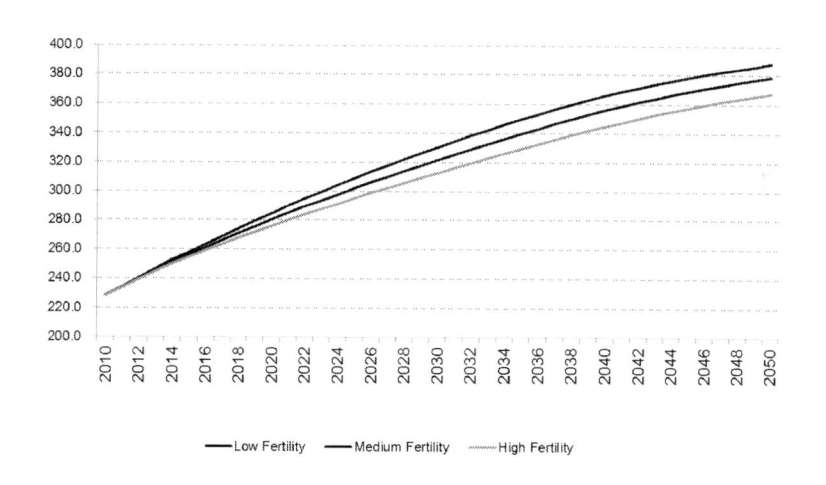

Source: HCF

Resource availability: Is there enough?

Before progressing to shorter term considerations, we might just pause and consider resources, for many people are agitated by the thought of the world becoming exhausted – literally. The world might run out of resources. Virgin resources are obviously a finite entity, but this ignores recyclability. The forecasts of exhaustion have always proved false. The British economist Jevons "proved" in the 19th century that the UK would run out of coal, that there was no answer to this and that industrialisation would falter, stop and reverse. He proved to be an industrial Malthus. He ignored the possibility of new resources in countries yet to be explored and of alternatives, especially oil. Similarly, oil forecasters have always seen resources being exhausted in approximately 30 years. At the time of my forecast of steel demand growth, known reserves of iron ore will be exhausted before 2050.

These doom scenarios are a function of the failure to understand economics and technology, not the reality of the natural world. Oil reserves like all other geological commodities are defined in relation to the price of the product. If the price is insufficient to cover the full costs of production then the company owning the resources is not allowed to classify them as reserves, they must remain as resources. These regulatory restraints are to protect investors from unscrupulous financiers. They are a function of exploration expenditures used to prove out reserves. At a distance of more than 30 years it is not worth doing this – so reserves have always had a finite limit. This finite limit however is movable depending on demand and price.

In the case of iron ore, exploration is well developed. Exhibit 5.8 provides a January 2013 table from the United States Geological Survey. This shows currently known reserves of ore by country, in tonnes of ore and iron content. The iron content is well short of that likely to be required by 2050 at 80bn. However resources for the US alone are stated to be 27bn of iron, in addition to the 2.1bn of reserves. The grade of iron content is less than in the reserves, which leads to it being more expensive to process – hence not qualifying today as reserves. There is no absolute shortage of virgin iron.

EXHIBIT 5.8: WORLD MINE PRODUCTION AND RESERVES

Country	Mine Production/Mtpa		Reserves/Mt	
	2010	2011	Crude Ore	Iron Content
Australia	433	480	35,000	17,000
Brazil	370	390	29,000	16,000
Canada	37	37	6,300	2,300
China	1,070	1,200	23,000	7,200
India	230	240	7,000	4,500
Iran	28	30	2,500	1,400
Kazakhstan	24	24	3,000	1,000
Mauritania	11	11	1,100	700
Mexico	14	14	700	400
Russia	101	100	25,000	14,000
South Africa	59	55	1,000	650
Sweden	25	25	3,500	2,200
Ukraine	78	80	6,000	2,100
USA	50	54	6,900	2,100
Venezuela	14	16	4,000	2,400
Other Countries	48	50	12,000	6,000
Total	2,590	2,800	170,000	80,000

Source: USGS and Hatch

Of greater significance is the recyclability of steel. This has been mentioned before but needs to be more detailed here. Eventually all, or nearly all of steel production will use scrap. Scrap is infinitely recyclable – it represents a reserve of iron units limited only by how much steel is currently in use. The major constraint on its use is that it needs to be sourced from obsolete uses. This requires time and represents a cost. The rule which has always proved useful to estimate the pool of useable scrap available in an economy is that of 70/17. Available obsolete scrap is 70% of apparent steel consumption, including net trade in steel products, 17 years before. Obsolete material depends on the cycle of use; tin cans are 6 months, domestic appliances

2-5 years, cars 10–15 years etc. Similarly, for capital equipment, buildings are 25–50 years and infrastructure 50–100 years. By taking into account the applications we can arrive at a 17-year average. The price of scrap determines the amount actually recovered from the scrap available. As steel demand growth levels off, the available pool gets closer to the current use of steel, and as iron ore gets more expensive - as it will - the recovery rate will increase. The attractiveness of the EAF scrap based process is reinforced by its capital efficiency and flexibility: hence my belief that by 2050, about 44% of steel will be produced via the EAF using scrap as a raw material. This percentage will gradually rise through the balance of the century.

Resources which are technologically inaccessible are not qualified as reserves. Resource demand also depends on technology. For example, eventually there will be a cheap way of making titanium metal and this could reduce the demand for nickel and chrome in stainless steel and lead to an explosion of demand for titaniferrous raw materials. The list of examples is endless. What is predictable is that the notion of "exhaustion" is false; what is not predictable is how this will be the case.

CHAPTER SIX

Is there growth after China?

> *"The key to successful change is sensitivity towards that which is indigenous and, in the long run, diversity will always be more resilient than monocultures". Jonathan Watts*

China is changing

The Chinese growth story is not finished but it has reached a turning point. The boom period is ended. Whilst growth will continue, it will not be at rates of 20% p.a. It is already at a slower pace, and in diversified industries reflecting a more consumer-driven economy, growth in finished steel usage will be slowing. The rates of growth may still remain the envy of the developed world! However, the Chinese story is much more complex than just a slowing whilst maintaining a steady direction. The future direction has some major difficulties; and the past was based on a major strategic mistake which will permanently damage the Chinese steel industry profitability; but further growth and development is firmly based if unlikely to be fast or substantial. The story of the next 15 years and beyond is not likely to be as most pundits assume. To begin with, we need a little history.

An historical mistake

When Deng made the biggest decision of a thousand years, to go for economic growth using the tools of capitalism and to scrap Maoist delusions, the Chinese government knew this would require mammoth quantities of steel and hence; even more quantities of iron ore. Initially, it was envisaged that this would be supplied locally. Little was known of the scale and quality of local iron ore supply but it was vast in the context of Chinese steel production in 1979 which was less than 20Mt p.a. Anyway, if seaborne ore was required, large reserves were coming into production in Brazil and Australia at low cost – there would be no problem. We must bear in mind that at this time China was an internationally isolated country and had been for 500 years, since the decision of the then emperor to destroy all deep sea shipping because China had nothing to learn from the outside world. Decisions were driven by a lack of exposure to and respect for foreign experience. Even relations with Russia were strained and confrontational, with low-level armed conflict in central Asia.

The issue of iron ore supply was left to take care of itself but the growth of Chinese demand changed the rules of the market totally. Now seaborne supply lagged behind demand and prices surged. Chinese reserves proved to be costly and poor. But the Chinese foresaw no difficulty as the country was the largest customer globally and so they expected to control the market. It turned out not to be so easy; despite three years of effort and non-comprehension. Contract discussions consisted of little more than uncomprehending Chinese repeating demands for low prices:

"Why can I not have the low price I want – we are the biggest countrywide consumer?"

"Because we will not sell at that price and your producers will buy from us anyway, at the price we offer" ... and so on.

The Chinese had misunderstood how markets work, but then they had no, or little, experience.

So the approach was changed: if the country could not beat the suppliers it would join them and swamp the supply, thereby creating the means to drive down the price anyway. Some $20-30bn has been invested in iron ore ventures and stakes for little value. Poor quality assets have been acquired with inadequate due diligence. Project costs and timescales have escalated due to inexperience in construction in foreign jurisdictions and, again, lack of due diligence. Finally, where product has emerged, its value in use has been less than expected and higher priced seaborne quantities from the big three iron ore producers are still better value even at their prices. There is one exception to this, which is Chinalco's investment into Simandou which represents a change of approach; relying on one of the majors to deliver a high quality project and participate by the provision of finance.

If China had not been locked into narrow, closed, thinking it would have learnt from Japan and ensured that iron ore capacity expansion, at quality and low cost, and with their influence, preceded steel growth. But then it is hard to envisage China being willing to learn and especially from Japanese experience given the conflicts of the 20th century. The die is now cast and China's integrated blast furnace steel industry is forever a high-cost industry. The subject of my first trip to China in 1993 was exactly this subject and one could see the inevitable rail crash from that distance.

China knows it has an industry whose competitiveness is compromised by the above mistakes. It will not compete successfully in the international market and so China will never become a structured net steel exporter, it will only export for short periods of time on the occasion of global economic discontinuities. Furthermore, the future of steel use needs to be in value added and not steel intensity. How long will China need to be the shipbuilder to the world?

The demographic time bomb

We have seen the issue from an earlier chapter. China is in a race against time to get its population to a high standard of living. Already the employment pool is shrinking. This emphasises the need for higher and higher labour value-added. This puts a premium on steel consolidation, rationalisation and modernisation which will now come quickly; and it also reinforces the position of the large-scale quality iron ore producers as higher quality ores make the production of high-quality steel easier and cheaper. There is still scope for growth in steel volumes, for a high labour productivity society is a steel-intensive one as machines, in the broadest sense, enhance this. Agriculture needs more capital and equipment and urbanisation has a long way to go. As we know from the UK and USA, service-intensive economies are not "steel light". The growth will be moderate and China is unlikely to consume, at home, a billion tonnes of steel in a year.

A financial crash is coming!?

There is a growing anxiety breaking out in the West about the over-borrowing in the Chinese banking sector; even more about the unknown levels in the shadow banks. The official banks now have assets between $24–25trn, which is twice the GDP. This has ballooned since the global financial crisis in 2008 and there has been a construction boom to end all booms, with the expectation that much of that is economically unjustified. If these conditions existed in the West, then there would be a catastrophic collapse in asset values. Credit tightening would occur from the centre, some loans would not be re-financeable when they became due, with write-downs and bankruptcies to follow and the threat of a chain-reaction meltdown. This is the threat that existed in 2008 in London and New York.

Now the doomsters are forecasting the same in China with economic disruption, unemployment and a massive recession. But there is a great big difference in circumstances. Banking is a game of mirrors and confidence. Write-downs can be accommodated if the institution can itself be refinanced. This is what avoided the crisis and converted it into no more than a problem in 2008. Governments, at least in the US and UK provided the capital for bank refinancing. For us this was done by quantitative easing, or "kicking the can down the road" but the Chinese are in a much stronger position: whilst the UK and USA are net debtors, China is a net creditor. It can use its foreign reserves and gold reserves to support the banking system. These are estimated at $4trn. After that there is also quantitative easing.

So there will be a correction as asset prices are brought back to reality and this will cause a difficulty in the near term – in the next two years. But, there will be no financial meltdown.

Life after China

Other developing countries are still in an early high-growth phase, though only one is widely recognised as such: India. This has been achieving growth rates for the economy as a whole of 7% and steel growth has followed, production nearly doubling in the last 10 years. There is much more to come, but without China's central drive from an authoritarian regime, growth will be slower and more sporadic. The other BRICs, Brazil and Russia, are relatively small with a combined population of only 300 million. Their contribution to steel demand will never be dramatic compared to the two population giants of China and India. After the BRICs there is a host of other countries aspiring to increased living standards. These countries are mostly smaller. The next 1.3bn people, equivalent to China's population, are in 11 different countries. We will examine later how these will meet their steel consumption requirements; their complexity will enable the dawn of a new era for steel industry structure, but the industry will need to seize the opportunity.

The next five years

For this period there is likely to be a surplus of supply capacity over demand. Estimates of overcapacity vary with lows of 300Mt and highs of 500Mt. However it will be only a short time before this surplus is eroded by demand growth. Current demand of 1.5bn growing at 4% generates an extra demand of 325Mt in five years. Bearing in mind that the industry requires there to be a buffer of "overcapacity" of 15% to allow for the avoidance of extreme shortages and to accommodate the business cycle, then the 500Mt surplus disappears in four years. If the surplus is only 250Mt, it disappears in one year. We will soon be out of the dismal years as long as growth in capacity has more or less halted for the time being. The greatest question is thus: will capacity continue to increase and if it does, at what rate? Worldsteel currently forecasts rates of new capacity of between 1 and 2% p.a.; after adjusting for retirements of capacity this implies a net reduction.

As I write this in January 2014, the mood of depression is deep but the signs of recovery are already appearing, with USA capacity utilisation hovering around 78% and prices beginning to revive on both sides of the Atlantic. The general view is that this growth will be generated mostly by the BICs, excluding Russia, plus cyclical recovery in developed markets. China will continue to add demand, maybe 200Mt over the next 10–15 years. India will add 40–50Mt over the next five years, with a modest contribution from Brazil, and elsewhere the surplus will dissolve rapidly. Certainly, it will have dissolved long before the time any coordinated industry-wide initiative to eliminate "surplus capacity" can be implemented. As so often, the industry is in danger of focusing on solving yesterday's problem to the detriment of taking advantage of tomorrow's opportunity.

Capacity expansion will depend on China, like so much else for the next five years. If China begins a serious consolidation phase then this will bring with it a closure of uneconomic and environmentally distressing capacity. This will more than compensate for capacity expansion elsewhere. In my view this will happen over this period.

20/20 vision

Looking forward to 2050, there is no "next China or India". Indonesia is the next most populous country after China and India, at 240 million. When we are looking at the development of steel demand and supply for "the next China", that is the countries coming after the BRICs, we are looking to 11 different countries to accumulate 1.3bn people. These countries are in the chart (Exhibit 6.1) below, plus the next nine, with some key facts pertaining to our subject of steel.

EXHIBIT 6.1: THE 20/20 COUNTRIES AND THEIR STEEL USE

Country	Population/M 2012	Population/M 2050	Iron Ore Production /ktpa	Iron Ore Reserves/ Mt Metal Content	Steel Production, 2011/Mt	Steel Consumption 2011/Mt	Steel ASU* kg/cap	Economy – Average Real Growth Rate 2010 – 2012/%	2012 GDP PPP** US$'000/ cap.
Indonesia	241	321	27	-	3.6	13.1	53.5	6.2	5.0
Pakistan	173	271	150	-	0.85	2.5	14.1	3.3	2.9
Nigeria	160	440	16	-	0.1	1.9	12.4	7.5	2.7
Bangladesh	151	202	13	-	-	2	12.8	6.3	2.0
Mexico	118	156	7,722	400	18.1	20.1	183.5	4.5	15.3
Philippines	93	157	1,082	-	1.2	5.9	58.3	6.0	4.3
Vietnam	89	104	530	-	4.9	12.1	133.8	5.9	3.5
Ethiopia	87	188	-	-	-	-	-	7.5	1.2
Egypt	78	122	100	-	6.5	8.6	104.8	3.0	6.6
Iran	75	101	13,000	1400	13.2	21.4	315.8	2.3	13.1
Turkey	72	95	2,400	-	34.1	28.7	364.3	6.9	15.0
Thailand	66	62	500	-	4.2	17	255.1	4.5	10.0
DRC	62	155	-	-	-	-	-	7.1	0.4
Myanmar	52	59	2,729	-	0.025	1.2	25.1	5.7	1.4
S. Africa	52	63	38,500	650	7.5	5.9	120.1	2.9	11.3
Colombia	46	63	96	-	1.3	3.4	75.9	4.7	10.7
Ukraine	46	34	44,300	2300	35.3	7.5	166.5	3.2	7.6
Tanzania	45	129	-	-	-	0.4	10.4	6.6	1.7
Kenya	41	97	7	-	0.02	1.2	30.2	5.1	1.8
Argentina	40	51	-	-	5.6	6.1	145.7	6.9	18.2
Total	1,787	2,870							

*ASU: Apparent Steel Use, **PPP: Purchasing Power Parity; Source: worldsteel, UN, USGS, CIA and Hatch

These countries are the 20 largest countries in the developing world by population, excluding the BRICs. I have chosen to headline this section 20/20 as I believe these 20 countries will constitute the major area of growth for the next 20 years. Far too little attention is paid to the exciting prospect of their development for steel.

How the demand in these countries will be met is a complex question. Their fragmentation adds complexity; there will be no consistent answer. Looking at the chart reveals some interesting observations. In total, the list accounts for 1.8bn people, 27% of the global total. By 2050 the forecast is that they will account for 2.8bn, then about 30% of the total. Of these countries 12, or 60%, have recorded an average GDP growth rate of more than 5% for the last three years: a rate of growth to be envied by the developed world and which, if continued, will have dramatic long-term consequences.

The average GDP per head, at purchasing power parity to the US dollar, varies enormously, from $400 in the DRC, to $18,000 in Argentina. The median, unadjusted for population, is $6,700: already two-thirds of the global average. A 5% growth rate in GDP over the next 37 years, to 2050, will bring this number to $25,000, adjusted for the increase in population. This is the expected world average in 2050. This is greater, by 150%, than the equivalent Chinese number today, which is approximately $10,000. For reference, that of the USA is approximately $50,000. This group of 20 has a steel consumption per person today of 88 kg per year and total steel use is 157.7Mt, with production of 136.5Mt. The steel intensity of India today is 68kg per head. At $25,000 per head, their steel intensity to GDP ratio is likely to be approximating to a developed country today. If this is 400kg per person in TSU then the total demand will be 1.2bn tp.a.

The next 15 years, indeed the next 50 years, will be much more than just the maturation of China and the growth of India, with the other BRICs playing a minor role. The next 20 countries represent an opportunity for steel more than one and a half times the size of India or equivalent to China 15 years ago; at the time I presented my incredible scenario to the AISI, Chinese annual production was 100Mt. These countries already have a steel demand more than that of India: twice in total volume and 20% more per head. Over the next 15 years these countries can expect to double their combined GDPs and they are now at an inflection point for steel, whereby their growth in demand is likely to be at a rate between one and a half and twice their GDP growth. This indicates that their combined demand for steel, in 2028, will be 600Mt not the 158 as at present: a 10% compound growth. They represent a similar growth opportunity to that of China 15 years ago.

The industrial development models and patterns they choose to follow to meet this need are not going to be as simple as that chosen by China.

Infinite variety

Like Cleopatra, these countries exhibit infinite variety, which is their charm to the observer or the tourist, but makes envisaging their futures challenging, and all the more interesting for that. Geographical diversity is obvious but this is complemented by religious variability. Their cultures include ones with predominantly Buddhist, Muslim, Hindu, Christian and also very mixed religious affiliations. Politically there are countries with relatively strong democratic roots and others with highly authoritarian histories and predilections. Many are politically highly volatile and suffer severe political upheavals involving military coups followed by periods of democracy; witness Pakistan, Egypt etc. Sovereign risk is perceived as high – but is trending downwards; if only slowly. The average country risk factor for the 20 countries I have highlighted has declined by 0.25 out of a total score of 10, over the last 10 years. . No country has the homogeneous and centralised structure of a China and in total they have more combined heterogeneity than India itself.

Their steel industries, where they exist, are similarly variable and often have a state ownership background. Ukraine shares the Russian communist past. In the role of the state as an investor, there is a similar unhappy experience, with only the exceptions of South Africa (with Iscor) and Turkey (with Erdemir) representing examples of, at least, limitedly successful state ownership. Iscor was modestly successful, although like so many state industries it was over-manned and bureaucratic when privatised to Mittal Steel. Erdemir was successful and more efficient. In the cases of, for example, Nigeria, Indonesia, Philippines, and Pakistan, the experience of state involvement has been negative with losses, inefficiency and poor technology predominating. A number of countries have already privatised their state-owned steel assets including Ukraine, Philippines, Turkey, South Africa, Argentina and Mexico, and some of these have anyway had significant private investment alongside the state. One country with substantial production, Thailand, has always been only private. Foreign participation has been relatively open and substantially more so, with the exception of Ukraine, than in the case of any BRIC country.

One very important feature which differentiates this group of 20 from the BRICs is that none of them have ever shown any significant desire for geo-political dominance or influence. Countries that have these desires have seen steel, until very recently, as a key component in achieving political objectives. This has led to a policy of strong state involvement in the steel sector. For the 20, this does not apply.

These countries have choices as to how they will seek to develop their steel supply in terms of ownership, the physical location of production and the structure of supply chains. These choices will impact on the opportunities they represent for current companies in the steel sector. But the greatest concern for current steel players is the perceived danger of overcapacity and unfair competition which is a question of the part the state will play in funding development and protecting it from competition. The role of the state, as so often in the steel sector, is crucial to the economic and financial future of the industry, locally and globally. The model of state involvement is not a simple choice in itself and there are several examples from which to learn.

Models of steel development

There have been different models used by different regions and, as always, we should look to the past to identify what patterns of development have been chosen, as these will be the ones available when governments and other organisations consider their future options. I offer the reader a warning: my considerations are forced to be summarised and simplified. Despite that, I think they are useful in identifying alternatives and highlighting what mistakes have been made that can be avoided in future. So what are these models? The big centres of steel production are USA, EU, Japan, Russia, Brazil, India and of course last but not least, China. Each of these has followed a different path.

Forced industrialisation

The Soviet model was just this. Industrial targets for everything were set by central planning through Gosplan and success was defined as delivery against these, whether or not the products were used or desired by anything other than the plan. Industrial structures tended to be highly integrated to take advantage of the perceived benefits of coordination; those of competition being ideologically forbidden. So, certainly at the end of the Soviet period, products such as tractors, for example, would be produced in plants integrated backwards as far as steel and raw material production. There would be insufficient demand to take the products and the surplus would be fed back directly into the steel furnaces after sitting in a large finished inventory. This structure was deliverable without critical comment because of the monolithic nature of the Soviet state apparatus and the totalitarian political history of Russia. Russia also has a geography and geology which holds abundant resources of raw material and energy. It could avoid dependency on international trade. This was a state-ownership model but I don't regard it as state capitalism as the role of both the consumer and capital markets were eradicated and substituted by planning.

Amazing as it now seems, this model was seen as viable and admired by many in the West for decades. It collapsed under the weight of its own ineffectiveness in 1989/90 and I doubt that any country will now follow this model in hope of economic success.

State capitalism

This is the Chinese model. Targeting here was more sophisticated that in the Soviet system. The aim was economic growth and employment, not just industrialisation and collectivisation. The consumer or population in general was central to the approach: the first aim was to employ, feed and house them; the second to switch to satisfaction of other aspirations. The ultimate aim has been the preservation of communist party rule; unlike in Russia, recognition was made that the well-being of the general public needed to be met. The complexity of the Chinese system required a high level of regional discretion, but with central direction at important times and on important topics. I see China's central government recognising this and choosing to focus only on 10% of issues, but the most critical 10% at any one time. The existence of a mandarin tradition, totally absent in Russia, provided the managerial means to achieve success. Capitalism was allowed: Deng said, "It is glorious to be rich", but within strict limits.

Regulated entrepreneurialism

This is the Indian model. The extreme complexity of India has not allowed central planning, despite the Russian influence in India through the 1950s and 60s in the heyday of apparent success for Soviet Russia. India is the most complex country in the world, every religion is here and many different languages. Several great civilisations have ruled here, but none monolithically. Neither Mogul nor British rule was ever total or homogeneous. The written culture of India is older than any other, including China. The variety of interests required a structure of regulation over most aspects of public and economic life, and the legacy of the Raj provided this. The central authority is exercised through regulation and it operates through constraints rather than plans. But the innate dynamism, complexity and deep intelligence of Indian culture means that entrepreneurialism is the dominant economic model, even if often exhibited through Maharajah-like family empires: an historical model of success being reused. Thus state ownership in steel has never been dominant and the first steel company was Tata's, a private venture developed in the teeth of opposition from British interests and with the assistance of US technologists and managers in the late 19th century.

As a very wise gentleman with a long and intimate involvement with the Indian steel industry, as well as experience of China, told me: "You must understand that in China they have order but no law and here in India we have law but no order." This explains much that is different about the two systems.

Market capitalism

This is the model of the USA. This is the "classic" capitalist model which is often derided by statists such as France as "Anglo-Saxon". It has been remarkably successful. It has outlasted other models, is becoming dominant and will be the only model by the end of the century as it places demand - the consumer, the ultimate reason for economic activity - at the centre. Here entrepreneurs initiate and create in all industries and often arise from outside the industry they change. In steel, perhaps the two greatest were Andrew Carnegie and Ken Iverson. The corporations they create are funded by private capital at birth and progress to public capital markets.

Entrepreneurialism gives way to managerialism over time as scale breeds a focus on managing internal processes as a key to improvement, and success breeds complacency. This is still dominated by the market but the inherent institutional inertia of managerial capitalism introduces a long period of decline when growth begins to slow. The economic functions these managed businesses perform are eventually taken over by new entrepreneurs, demonstrating the Schumpeterian model of "creative destruction"; a key aspect of this model, exhibited in steel by the decline of US Steel (Carnegie) and the growth of Nucor (Iverson). The model works better than any other as it puts the market at the centre and has its own built-in virtuous circle through creation replacing decay replacing creation. Market capitalism benefits from the same characteristic that Churchill ascribed to democracy: "Democracy is the worst form of Government except all those other forms that have been tried from time to time."

State-supported oligopoly

This is the Brazilian option whereby the state facilitates industrial development by participating but is not exclusive and allows a number of private ventures to flourish. The private sector is not as open and free as in the USA, because the families that control these ventures are dominant. Public capital markets are available and used but are subservient to the oligopolistic families, through differential share structures and banking relationships. There is a happy coincidence of interests between the state and capital enterprises – mutual support is the way of expressing this. Oligopoly can be traced back to the colonial influence in all countries having an Iberian-influenced past. Both Iberian colonisers were still feudal at the time of their empires and feudalism is intensely oligopolistic.

Brazil had, for a time, direct state involvement which did create the early steel industry – CSN, which was established before the Second World War. After it, starting in the 1960s, CVRD grew out of the vision of one man and the capital support of the state. Eventually this was privatised and the pieces fell under the continuing influence of the state, as with Vale, or under that of key families, such as the Gerdau group or

CSN. Foreign participation was and is allowed, hence ARBED's (now ArcelorMittal) involvement from the 1920s and Nippon Steel's participation in Usiminas. This has been a very sophisticated approach, but not without its limitations. The inherent oligopolistic nature leads to inefficiencies: hence rebar prices are always significantly higher in Brazil than the rest of the world. These things are dampeners on other sectors' growth ambitions, and on innovation throughout the economy – it is difficult for Schumpeter to operate. Oligopolistic structures always inhibit the overall achievement of the economy. There is a sense in which Brazil is "a country of the future – and always will be", as Stefan Zweig famously said. Brazil never quite seems to fulfil its economic promise, which is a comment on its chosen model of development.

Japan is a variant of this model. The role of the family groups is taken by the Keiretsu. The state is not a direct participant in ownership but is very much a facilitator and guider of development, prioritising between groups, ensuring coordination in supply chains and a balance of interests between capital, consumers and employees. This is all assisted by the savings habits of Japanese individuals, who have a high savings rate and no propensity to invest abroad whether in shares or bonds. This provides captive capital at low rates of expected interest. The Keiretsu and other corporate entities, do invest overseas to support their market ambitions and their productive assets back in Japan. The absence of raw material resources (not just for steel) has placed a premium on quality of product and efficiency in production as international comparative advantages.

The hybrid

This is Europe and I have failed to come up with a categorisation better than seeing Europe as a hybrid of all the above models. This is a reflection of the inherent complexity of Europe itself. Eastern Europe was for 45 years controlled ruthlessly by the Soviet system and still bears its legacy, although this is rapidly disappearing. The French approach to capitalism can at best be called "ambiguous". The German is highly coordinated and looks quite oligopolistic. Italy is a form of the Brazilian model. Britain is rather like India – not surprising as the British Raj was one of the building blocks of that country - although with less regulation. Being inherently a country built on trade and empire, we borrow avidly from everyone.

Each of these models - and I don't pretend they are without a degree of ambiguity in themselves - I find useful as heuristic tools. They exhibit different combinations of a few elements: the role of the state either through planning or regulation; the role of private enterprise either through entrepreneurialism or managerialism; competition as open or partially controlled through oligopoly etc. The model chosen by any country will largely be a function of the culture, modified through interpreted global experience, the interpretation being done by the administrative and political elites.

Resource availability

Resource availability and access to them has been a major conditioning factor on the models chosen and their success. Whatever the ideological and cultural prejudices of the political elite might be, there have to be the tools available, natural resources being one such tool, to implement the chosen model. Not all countries are born equal, nor can they become equal as to resources. In all the above cases raw materials were available to be exploited – except in Japan. Japan went out and created new sources of raw material in Australia and less so in Brazil; resources which, because of their scale and quality, provided an advantage to the Japanese steel producers who emphasised this by building steel plants on the coast to reduce the logistical cost of imports.

The UK was the first country to industrialise, and it can be a subject of endless debate why this was so, but without the resources of iron ore and coal it would have been impossible. The Netherlands was in advance of the UK as a trading country and a source of industrial innovation by the middle of the 17th century, yet 100 years later it was a backwater by comparison. There are various reasons for this, but it might not be purely coincidental that the Netherlands lacks raw materials for steel production. In the early days of industrial development there was no, or very little, trade in raw materials across international borders. All the cases above, except Japan, have a high degree of self-sufficiency in physical resources, which enabled them to develop. These resources might not last very long, as in the UK, or be economically competitive, as in China – but they existed.

Capital is also a resource needed to build any industry. The UK had its imperial territories which generated much surplus which was brought back to the UK and invested in enterprises. The sugar of the West Indies, for example, was a hugely profitable industry for several generations and was much fought over by the French and British for that reason. With the early development of the City, and the establishment of banking, especially the Bank of England in 1694, it was possible to channel agricultural profits from large estates into various enterprises, local and international. American industries benefitted from UK investment as did other countries such as Argentina. Russia and China were able to use state capital as their populations had limited expectations from the state for social, health and educational expenditures. They could also enforce saving levels through taxation, non-disbursement of income and restricted credit. Japan had a high local savings level and a lack of any propensity to invest such savings abroad.

Although steel remains a foundation industry and its availability is critically important to the development of other industries, there are now a multitude of industries available for investment and seeking funds. With the continuing opening up of capital flows and globalisation generally, the capital for the emerging 20 will be provided both locally and internationally. But capital will be available as it always is if investments look attractive, and if the rule of law prevails to protect investors and give them confidence that their investments will generate returns that they can access.

The models discussed above provide materials for any country to craft a development model, but which model will be followed? That is the subject for the next chapter.

CHAPTER SEVEN

The growth model for the next 20

"Every sentence I utter must be understood not as an affirmation, but as a question". Nils Bohr

The factors influencing the choice

There are certain conditioning factors which will impact the policy-makers in these 20 countries and elsewhere. These factors are: cultural predisposition, raw material availability, market size driven by population and capital availability. Experience has shown that state ownership and centralised planning have only a limited role in successful development. The market must be relied on, and the state should be restricted to, regulation and not direction.

Capital availability will be limited. Forced saving on the Chinese model is not going to be possible in the new information age: the people will not allow themselves to be deprived of the benefits of growth for long. Also the expansion, even explosion, of demands for health, education and social welfare place demands on state budgets which deprive them of the ability to deploy much capital in industry. They will choose to deploy it when available into infrastructure.

Natural resources for steel are not plentiful in the 20 countries I have under consideration. Reliance on seaborne trade is inevitable for most supply for most countries. This trade is likely to be at all points of the value chain, not just in raw materials as has been the case for such as China.

The market scale of many of the countries will not justify major steel works using blast furnace technology, at least for a considerable time, until a great deal more development has occurred. The reverse applies in the BRICs. The use of EAF scrap routes will be limited by the lack of scrap until later, towards 2050, and by the tendency for scrap to be used in markets where it is generated.

Finally, culture conditions decisions, especially political culture. I have commented on the lack of desire of most of these countries to play big roles on the geo-political stage. Steel is not a strategic industry for most.

The existence of raw materials was a precursor for all the countries developing steel sectors, except for Japan. The raw materials may have been poor in quality and not competitive on cost but they existed. It was the mechanisms for the provision of capital which varied. The raw materials gave these countries the freedom to deploy capital according to their own cultures – 'culture' meant in the widest sense of the accumulated political, social and intellectual capital available. Hence different patterns of state involvement as to ownership and regulation exist. The overwhelming experience now, and part of the intellectual capital of all emerging and developing countries, is that state involvement as shareholders is detrimental to a healthy steel sector. The experience of communism has led to the withdrawal, through privatisations, of state ownership in many of the 20 developing countries.

There is one important caveat to this thesis that state ownership is in retreat everywhere and will no longer be an option for steel developments on anything other than a very modest scale. There needs to be available pools of sufficient funding, whether private or public, to meet the capital requirements of steel within the political timescales and ambitions of the country. China lacked these pools and its desired speed of development did not allow time for them to emerge. There are such pools in capitalist countries, but instruments to use them need to be developed.

In addition we should consider the earlier observations about aging populations. The demands on the public purse are rising. Government borrowing levels are rising and not just in the developed world. The percentage of GDP now represented by government debt for the 20 is an average of 40%. The flexibility available to governments for the deployment of capital as they see fit is declining. In all ways governments no longer have the ability they had a generation or two ago, to fund major industrial development initiatives. It is not only the tide of economic understanding that has ebbed away from state ownership and will not return but also the tide of available means.

Rejuvenate the Japanese model for the future

The case of Japan is different from the other centres of steel and provides an interesting perspective. Japan has no raw materials for steelmaking. After the Second World War the victorious allies were unsure about how to let Japan develop. It had been quite industrialised before 1942. Indeed, it was a trade dispute about steel scrap exports from the USA to Japan which had helped to trigger the outbreak of war, although the causes ran deeper. After the war, the question of reindustrialisation, or not, was a real one; this was settled by pragmatic circumstance. Japanese production was required to help supply forces fighting in Korea in the early 1950s when the rise of communist China was a perceived threat. A thriving capitalist Japan would be a symbol of success to put against the appeal of communism in Asia.

Direct state ownership was not an option as the USA would not have allowed it even if the Japanese had wanted to choose that – but they did not need to. Japan had pools of capital through the high savings rate, and the expertise to deploy that capital successfully through the Keiretsu, successors of similar conglomerate structures from the pre-war era. They therefore followed their own trajectory. The need for imported raw materials transported by small-scale and expensive ships, before the building of Cape-size bulk shipping, placed an enormous burden on Japanese steel costs. Then opportunities and needs coincided between Brazil and Japan with the arrival of Dr Batista.

Japan recognised that they needed to build a globally competitive manufacturing industry which would export to pay for the importation of raw materials. These sectors would need low cost, high quality steel. This steel could not be produced with existing technologies operating at current economies of scale and utilising current modes of transport which were also small-scale and expensive. Without radical technical and structural change Japan could never compete with US industry. The role of Dr Batista was crucial. Here was a true industrial radical. Brazilian, but internationally educated, he had responsibility for developing CVRD with its massive iron ore resources including the new and vast reserves of Carajas. The time was the early 1960s.

To realise the value of the new iron ore fields would require long rail infrastructure, new ports and new customers. The quality of the ore was much superior to the locally sourced ores currently being used in Europe, as with China today. To capture the value of this ore would require lower transport costs than were then available with ships no larger than Panamax. Large bulk ore carriers were needed. This would require rail and port investment on a then unknown scale. A new raw material and steel industry had to be conceptualised and built. The benefits would be enormous, as not only would ore be available at lower cost, but the superior quality would enhance the attractiveness of the new BOF technology then replacing open hearths. The large capital investments would themselves represent profit opportunities: someone had to build the large carriers for example. So there were benefits all round.

Batista travelled to Europe to talk with the established seaborne ore dependent companies; he was greeted as an impractical visionary. It was all too difficult, involving cannibalising much established capital; it was expensive and risky, especially as it involved long-term commitments between entities in different countries with widely different sovereign risks. For the Europeans, "it would never happen".

So, Dr Batista travelled to Japan. The more he talked to the Japanese, the more enthusiastic they became. Here was the answer to the Japanese steel challenge. A supply structure could be modelled with low-cost, high-quality ore for the long term, and if they built their steel plants on the coast the ore could be fed directly into their furnaces. In addition, the need for the ships would provide added demand. They could build the ships and their construction industry could build the assets in Brazil and finally, they had the access to the capital. The Japanese did not want to be dependent on one source for ore, the implied monopsonistic power would be a major hurdle in the way of success. Geology came to their rescue in the Pilbara, Western Australia. Here, major ore resources had been discovered with similar challenges and opportunities to those facing CVRD. The Japanese formed joint ventures with the miners in Australia to bring these mines into production.

Joint ventures, but more limited, was the model in Brazil. Here, though, the larger population led to the government encouraging ventures in steel production for local and export supply. Nippon Steel (now NSSMC following the merger with Sumitomo Metals) and Kawasaki Steel (now JFE) invested. The Japanese model for steel development forms a prototype, requiring refinement and redefinition, for what is needed for the new wave of developing countries.

The feasibility of a new model

Whereas, most of our models are essentially autarkic - each country's industry is self-contained using local raw materials and capital, and competitive with each other - the Japanese story is truly global and cooperative. It also provides the basis for a new model for the emerging 20 we have identified above. The virtues of thinking and acting collaboratively and globally are that they breed interdependence and mutuality so that issues of competitive overcapacity and unfair competition are much less likely to occur: a desirable situation for the steel sector.

The capital markets in established economies are efficient at raising funds. To do so requires business models which can show a good, if cyclical, profit and return profile, after taking account of risk. Today the steel sector cannot do that and I will return to how that can be achieved in the next chapter. This is however a prerequisite to avoid the pitfalls of state funding.

Established steel producers are the best mechanisms to deploy these funds as they are efficient at transferring technology and managerial expertise. Trying to do so through new ventures is slow and wasteful, especially in developing countries. This is not to deny an earlier point that new technologies can often only be effectively introduced by new ventures or by ones from outside the established companies.

To avoid economically destructive unfair competition, it is not enough just to avoid state ownership. Selling product at less than cost can be a matter of ignorance as much as malice. In particular, ignorance about the prices in the market, and especially of what the price will be tomorrow and later. I will be tempted to sell below my cost today if I think two things: that my competitor may exit the market soon and leave me free to recoup losses by price rises later, or that prices will rise soon and before I have suffered unbearable loss. Price transparency today and futures curves for product prices into the medium term are means to alleviate this ignorance. Behaviour can then be tied to educated expectations. These tools are available in other metal commodity markets to good but not perfect effect. I discuss this point in much more detail in a later chapter.

Further structural stability can be achieved if the productive assets are subjects of joint ventures. Competitors who have shared mutual interests in some part of the value chain will think long and hard about predatory behaviour as it will damage some part of their assets as well as someone else's. Thus in aluminium, alumina refineries and aluminium smelters are often the subjects of joint ventures which share the risks involved and provide a meeting point for economic interests and sharing expectations.

In petrochemicals, such joint ventures are standard practice and highly successful in stabilising prices and providing legitimate means for communication about expectations.

These partially new ways of organising affairs in the ferrous sector require willingness on the part of participants to allow them to happen. I refer to both companies and governments. The start of steel is in raw materials and especially iron ore. Here the major ore producers in Australia have been open to joint ventures. There, the former Nippon Steel, JFE, POSCO and Baosteel all have minority investments in operating iron ore mines in the Pilbara. Brazil has been much more difficult to operate in, with resource nationalism being a major issue. The company that discovered Carajas, perhaps the most economically attractive new iron ore resource since 1945, was not Brazilian – it was US Steel. However, they were never allowed to have the economic benefit. In Australia it has been different. This country has a wide-open democracy with a sophisticated and educated electorate. It has a small population and no need to look for major sources of jobs. It recognises that the economic benefits to the wider society of natural resource exploitation flow from the tax take through employment as well as royalties and the multiplier effect through the economy in general.

Likewise, as we look down the value chain into iron and steelmaking, these assets will benefit from similar structuring; as long as political considerations allow them to arise and be implemented. Economic nationalism in general and resource nationalism in particular, have been great inhibitors in the past. This occurs when individual or sub-group interests meet national ignorance. The root cause of this nationalism is not nationalism at all, but the ability of individuals to grab ownership of the assets and extract a rent for their use, using political power and influence for their own selfish benefit. This is often self-defeating as the attempted "rent extraction" is out of proportion to the asset's value, so eliminating the possibility of exploitation. In countries with poorly developed systems of the rule of law, this also leads to instability in the ownership titles so increasing the risk to investments and again limiting the possibility of exploitation. When this phenomenon meets either autocratic government or democracies with poor levels of economic education and understanding, then the individual interests can predominate.

Fortunately, these forces of nationalism are in long-term decline. The sovereign risk perception of many developing countries is on the decline, democratic processes of government, if not perfect, are gaining popularity and economies are becoming more open. As examples of this, we can look at many of the countries in our list of 20. Not only has the role of state ownership declined, but foreign ownership of ferrous assets is growing; examples include ArcelorMittal in Ukraine and South Africa, Ternium in Mexico, MMK in Turkey (an unhappy experience and poorly thought through), POSCO in Indonesia, and Tata Steel in Thailand.

It was the availability of raw materials that also facilitated steel growth in the various regions examined earlier. In the case of the 20, many countries are resource-short. There is still the possibility of discovery of major new iron ore resources in some countries which have been poorly explored, but these possibilities are declining rapidly. Modern exploration techniques including magnetic aerial survey, and the growth of demand, with commensurate increases in exploration budgets, have led to a major growth in geological knowledge in recent years. The earlier table, Exhibit 5.8, shows that only Iran and Ukraine have known iron ore reserves in excess of 1bn tonnes; 18 countries appear to lack sufficient resources to justify indigenous exploitation for major steel production.

The emerging increased reliance on distant resources of ore place even more emphasis on the structures outlined above. They will also encourage the emergence of new patterns of physical integration of steel processes; or rather new patterns of de-integration and asset-sharing. The transport of raw materials and steel products, given their relatively low value, is of increasing importance in cost structures. Iron ore is one third waste by weight. Steel is zero waste. However, slabs and other semi-finished steel for rolling need reheating if transported to a distant mill, and hence this implies wasted heat, but hot rolled coil does not. New opportunities will emerge for the physical structure and location of steelmaking processes.

These will be reinforced by the virtues of sharing assets as steel markets grow from small demand – where demand does not justify large facilities - to larger and more mature demand. Of the 20, there are 10 which have demand less than 4Mt p.a. for all products. It would be attractive for these countries to arrange ventures involving steel production in a country with raw materials, sharing the investment with an established steel producer and perhaps another emerging economy, but importing semi-finished steel and finishing and processing that steel locally. These countries could facilitate their entrepreneurs taking minority stakes in the steel plant overseas and a majority stake in the processing plant at home; a major established steelmaker could take the reciprocal stakes. This model could extend to many more countries below the size of the 20. Indeed many smaller countries have iron ore reserves which could be developed this way to the benefit of themselves. The joint venture approach will apply for a long time to the 20 when we consider the complexity of steel shapes and qualities, and how they can be economically supplied, within their total demand.

Globalisation and steel

All I am suggesting here is that steel follows the overall trend to deeper integration globally: this is the meaning of globalisation. Economies are integrating as international economies of scale and differential comparative advantage can be more freely exploited as trade barriers decline. This is demonstrated by the key statistics on trade and capital flows. Exhibit 7.1 shows the percentage of trade as a percentage of global GDP for the last 35 years. The nadir of this was in 1986 at about 34%, the high was in 2008 at about 62%; note that the numbers combine imports and exports and so are double counting and should be halved to arrive at trade as a % of world GDP. The Global Financial Crisis led to a decline as economic activity fell and trade suffered disproportionately, as it normally does in a recession. However, despite this and the continued recessionary environment in the developed economies, trade has started to grow again and is now only a half a percent below the peak.

EXHIBIT 7.1: GLOBAL TRADE AS A FRACTION OF GLOBAL GDP (%)

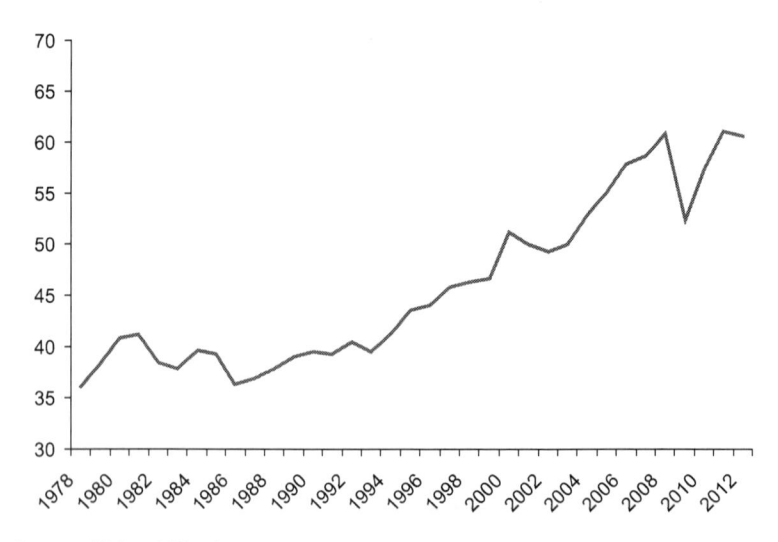

Source: UN and Hatch

Another aspect of globalisation is asset ownership. Today, cross-border ownership represents approximately 150% of world GDP. This has risen from the trough of almost zero in 1945 at the end of World War II. Assets held overseas had been liquidated, or confiscated, to fund the conflict. A peak had been reached just before World War I. This was when the UK held sway as the world's leading trade power and the gold standard was effectively guaranteed by the UK government. This guarantee is fundamental to capital flows. Without the benefit of global courts able to ensure and enforce ownership rights, investors need a reserve currency that they can escape to in times of tribulation.

When the Great Depression occurred, the UK was no longer able to act in this way as it was no longer a large, strong economy. The UK came off the gold standard in 1931. No country was willing to replace it and thus the Depression was extended as trade and investment continued to languish. After World War II, the USA took up the role and the dollar became the reserve currency and international cross-border investment began to recover. The dollar retains this role and it is desperately important that it continue to do so. A key requirement of a reserve currency is that the country providing it does not have any significant capital controls; if that freedom is taken away the reserve role is lost. For this reason, if for no other, the renminbi is not yet in a position to challenge the dollar.

This process of global integration will continue; it is another necessary condition for planning anything. Without it, the global economy will experience a very prolonged downturn, such as the Great Depression which, without the stimulus of World War II, might have continued for much longer. In the recent recession the reason for the avoidance of a depression, more than any other, was the continued existence of the role of the dollar. The integration of the global economy is a long-term stabilisation factor, as local interests become more and more identified with global ones.

The same will be true of steel if it can rise to the challenge of the next wave of steel-demand growth. Cross-border ownership of assets will help, but the bigger benefit will come from cross-border development of new assets to feed new demand. This will provide for better technology transfer, better construction and management, better coordination of demand and supply and better matching of individual enterprise interests with those of the industry as a whole.

Thus properly approached and conceptualised, the development of "the next China" in terms of demand presents a complex picture. It also presents a vista that represents a unique opportunity for current steel producers to participate for financial benefit and in ways which can avoid the diseases associated with state ownership and uncoordinated and competitive capacity expansion. However, whilst this opportunity requires some fundamental creative thinking and action, it also requires large amounts of capital which the private sector will and can only provide if there are clear opportunities for positive returns on that capital.

A modest proposal

I suggest for consideration a modest proposal of a way that the current steel companies could both assist the viable development of capacity required by the growth in demand I have identified and help to determine the conditions for their own success over the long term. I propose the formation of a Steel Development Bank.

This would serve to assist the development of viable enterprises in the 20 and beyond for the future. It would be funded initially by capital from current steel producers. Its brief would be to assist in the partial funding of bankable feasibility studies for steel making businesses and then construction where economically justified. No venture could be supported if it had a state capital in its shareholder register. The prefeasibility studies would have to be privately funded to avoid ideas which had little initial justification.

The bank would operate to a certain extent like the IFC but would take equity stakes in ventures. It would facilitate joint ventures between established and emerging companies. All supported ventures would have to commit to involving entities from more than 1 country in their equity structure. The bank would require that its financing entities had a right of first refusal over funding construction up to at least a strong minority level.

I suggest that an initial funding level of no more than maybe $250M would be required and this need not be vested at the start – it could be in committed funds to be drawn down as required. The staffing should be small maybe 10 and, certainly, not 100. Its existence would need to be guaranteed for a minimum of 5 years, and its overheads covered for that period, to give it the time to achieve some positive impact. The constitution of the bank would need to be carefully considered to provide independence but effective oversight. Clear criteria and conditions for investing funds would need to be delineated. I have here only provided a sketch of how it would operate.

The bank would be a tool to help create a healthy steel sector. It would be a positive and forward thinking approach and much more dynamic than the occasional calls for subsidies to help close capacity. It would be a clear attempt by the industry to seek to help itself and meet its own challenges without outside assistance.

In all circumstances, the improvement of returns for the industry is of critical and urgent importance. I will now turn my attention to the scale of funding required in the future and to the ways to make the steel sector financially viable.

CHAPTER EIGHT

Funding the growth

> *"Being good in business is the most fascinating kind of art."*
> Andy Warhol

The growth

I have envisaged a steel sector capacity of 4,550Mt p.a. by 2050. The capacity today is approximately 1,800Mt p.a.; that is 1,500Mt production and 300Mt of "overcapacity". This growth is driven largely by India and my top 20 following countries as detailed in the previous chapter. We may be expecting about 6,000Mt p.a. capacity by 2100. In this chapter, I will restrict my thoughts to 2050. The capital requirements for this growth are substantial. Steel is often referred to as a capital-intensive industry; it certainly requires large quantities of capital to build steel plants, especially integrated ones. EAF plants are cheaper. In the case of integrated plants there is, also, a commensurate and rising requirement for capital to fund mines and associated infrastructure. Just how much capital will need to be deployed and where it will come from is the subject of this chapter.

Some approximations

In addressing this very large topic over such a long period of time I will need to make some very large approximations. These are what are normally called "heroic assumptions". For example, there will be many technological advances and changes over this period in steelmaking and rolling. These are difficult to predict and impossible to model. So, whilst acknowledging that they will occur, I am willing to assume that they will have very little impact in reducing capital intensity. They may take a long time to proliferate and they may be balanced by increased capital requirements for, inter alia, environmental reasons. I will, therefore, be building my forecasts on existing technology.

I will also use current best practice costs. This is especially important for steel plants. There have been recent examples of extreme cost over runs such as with ThyssenKrupp in Brazil. I will ignore those possibilities. Also whilst infrastructure costs will be allowed for - in iron ore mining, items such as rails and ports - these will be ignored for steel capacity. The rationale is that steel plants will either be built at mine sites, port sites or near centres of population. In each case, the basic infrastructure costs will be met by other enterprises or the public sector in the name of general economic and societal development. On the whole, I think these are conservative assumptions in the sense of being at the low end of steel plant costs.

I will also ignore the benefits of reusing old but relocated plant. This does happen in the early stages of steel in developing countries when capital is short and labour is plentiful and cheap. However, in my experience, after dismantling, relocating and refurbishing, the benefits are modest. They are also very limited as to scope.

What products and processes?

Increased capacity of 2.75bnt of steel over the 37 years from 2013 is required. This provides for increased consumption of 2.46bnt. Not all will be greenfield and blast furnace. Capacity growth will be a mix of brownfield expansion and new greenfield, either EAF or blast furnace based. There will be capacity withdrawal as obsolete or non-economic plant is decommissioned. I will ignore the latter even though this will depress the amount of capital required. It is a complicating factor which is incalculable and steel plants have a habit of taking a long time to die. Again, a range of assumptions needs to be made. The EAF capacity will be a function of available scrap. Being less capital intensive, I assume it will be preferred to BF capacity whenever it is feasible. However, it will not be possible to use EAFs very much in countries which have rapidly emerging demand due to the slow process of steel obsolescence. As I have indicated previously, the rule of scrap availability in a mature economy is 70% of apparent steel consumption 17 years earlier. Allowing for the emerging market issue would reduce the use of EAFs but the availability of DRI (Direct Reduced Iron) can boost it; providing a virgin iron ore based feed for EAFs especially in areas with cheap gas. I shall treat these two factors as cancelling each other out. I will assume that EAF capacity in 2050 will be equivalent to the 70% of scrap availability. Apparent steel consumption growth from 2013 to 2050, I assume, will be a straight line function.

On the basis of the above, EAF capacity will be 1.96bnt in 2050. Today EAF production is approximately 500Mt but capacity exceeds that by an estimated 100Mt so the increase in EAF steelmaking capacity will be 1.36bnt by 2050. The residual increase will be met by BF capacity which is 1.39bnt. By 2050 EAF capacity will represent 43% of total capacity compared to 33% today. After 2050 if, as I expect, steel growth does slow, then EAF capacity will steadily increase as a percentage of the total.

What capital is needed?

Steel capacity expansion can be divided into three categories: incremental brownfield, new EAF and new BF. I assume 10% of all expansion is incremental and that costs about $200 /t. The EAF capacity costs $500 /t and BF costs $1000. These are reasonable assumptions but many variables are blended into these estimates. The greenfield costs are only up to the hot rolled stage and much demand is for value added product requiring further capital; particularly in flat rolled. To account for this, I assume an added $200 /t on a blended basis for the total product mix. None of these numbers cover the capital required for raw materials. The basis is that raw materials are delivered to the factory gate independently. So I have four categories of capital costs to accumulate:

1. Incremental steel capacity: 10% of 2.75bnt = 275Mt at $200 /t = $55bn
2. EAF new capacity: 90% of 1.36bnt = 1,224Mt at $500 /t = $612bn
3. BF new capacity: 90% of 1.251 bnt = 1,126Mt at $1000 /t = $1,126bn
4. Value adding capacity: 50% of 2.75bnt = 1.375bnt at $200 /t = $275bn

The total capital that has to be found at current prices for the required steel capacity increases is $2,068bn. Over 37 years, on a straight line basis, this is $56bn p.a. On current levels of production, this is $37 /t and this excludes capital required for maintenance of current capacity.

Capital for iron ore

The capital required for iron ore development is much more difficult to calculate than for steel-making. This is because these costs are driven by geology and geography not by technology. Anyone can build a steel plant, subject to planning and funding - it's just like a car assembly plant or, indeed, any other manufacturing facility. As long as you can secure supplies of raw materials and components, away you go. This is not so for iron ore or any other commodity such as oil or copper which are restricted by local geological conditions

The costs of extraction and bringing to market of commodities have an inbuilt tendency to rise, whereas, the opposite is the case for manufactured products. This was not always the case. For a century from the late 19th to the late 20th century, commodities' prices fell in real terms as did finished product prices: the former because of the discovery and development of massive rich, new deposits in the New World and other regions; the latter because of steady increases in yield efficiencies in the use of factors of production, as we have seen with steel. The latter process will continue, but not the former.

The geological world is now well explored and it will be a very big surprise if major new deposits of minerals are discovered, except those that are more expensive to extract than those already in operation: perhaps, subsea deposits. Commodity industries really are fundamentally different from manufacturing. Technology can have some impact on costs but these are overridden by more demanding geologies, longer and more difficult logistics and infrastructure and, most importantly, the gradual and steady decline in grades. There has been an irreversible sea change in the economic dynamics of raw materials costs in the last 15 years.

With this have come big changes in the capital cost of mines. Whereas in 2000 it might have cost $50 /t to increase capacity for iron ore in the Australian Pilbara, it now costs more than $100 /t. Nothing like this has happened in steelmaking. Thus, it is always likely that the capital costs for iron ore expansions will be underestimated.

Current iron ore capacity will deplete and some mines will become exhausted or the grades too poor to exploit, whilst others will survive on poorer resources which become reclassified into reserves as costs and prices increase. I will assume, somewhat arbitrarily, that 50% of current iron ore is exhausted and has to be replaced by greenfield reserves, whilst the other 50% can be saved through brownfield extension.

There are four calculations to take into consideration for capital for required iron ore capacity: new BF capacity, DRI capacity, pelletisation and replacement for depleted reserves.

New required BF capacity is 1,390Mt but nearly all steelmakers use some scrap in the furnace, anything from 0 to 25%. I will assume a 5% feed, which represents the home scrap generated within the steel plant itself and, thus, available for immediate recycling. Any higher percentage would deprive EAFs of feed and overly complicate my calculations for no benefit. The iron (Fe) content of the BF burden I will assume to be 62%. This is the quality used as a benchmark in China's seaborne trade. Iron ore varies greatly by Fe content but this is a reasonable basis for tonnage estimates. Thus the ore required for new BF capacity is: (1,390 x .95) / 0.62. The total is 2,130Mt. The capital needed for new iron mines can be highly variable. For Simandou (Guinea) the public stated expectation is for capital costs at $200-250 /t whilst at Minas Rio (Brazil) it will be in excess of that. These are the two largest greenfield projects currently under construction and the capital includes that required for infrastructure. I believe a reasonable estimate for iron mine capacity, including related infrastructure is $250 /t. The capital need for the above totally greenfield capacity is therefore $533bn. For depleting reserves there is a need for 800Mt at $250 /t for replacement and 800Mt at $100, this lower figure being for brownfield expansion. The combined total for iron ore mining to replace depleting assets is $280bn.

DRI material is used largely as a high quality complement to scrap. I believe this will grow by 200% over the period. In 2013 DRI use was approximately 60Mt so by 2050 it will be 180Mt and require a further 180Mt of suitable ore. This will be at a capital cost of $250 /t so requiring capital of $45bn.

There is the complication of pelletisation: all DRI material needs this, and ultrafine material for BF production, which will become more prevalent, mostly requires this processing. It is only possible to estimate the quantity that will be needed. I estimate that 30% of the new BF material, plus the DRI, will be pelletised. This totals 915Mt. Using a capital cost estimate of $150 /t, including necessary infrastructure, capital for pelletising will be $137bn.

So the sum total of capital needs is:

$533bn + $45bn + $280bn + $137bn = $995bn. Over 37 years this is $27bn p.a.

Can iron ore be funded?

The short answer is: yes. There are two sources of capital, excluding the state, which is undesirable and to be avoided if we want healthy and productive industries. Cash for capital investment can be generated from operations and can be provided by outside shareholders and lenders. The lending will only be forthcoming if the funders believe in the future profit prospects of the companies, in sufficient quantities to provide dividends or interest and to sustain and grow the business for the future.

Rio Tinto's annual results for 2013 contained the figures for its iron ore business which represents over 80% of its entire economic activity. For iron ore, attributable revenues were $26bn on 209Mt of shipments. Their operations mined more than that but the balance was owned by their partners. This represents revenues of $124 /t. Their shipments are approximately 13% of world production, but more when calculated as a percentage of seaborne trade. Rio Tinto has attractive and low operating cost assets so their EBITDA total was $17.5bn and their EBIT was $9.9bn. Shareholders need to be rewarded and interest paid to lenders, but these numbers show that certainly in 2013 Rio Tinto could afford to invest in iron ore. Indeed, if 50% of its EBIT was to be invested then at $250 /t they could add nearly 20Mt of capacity in one year alone.

The attractive economic fundamentals for iron ore are reflected in the market capitalisations of the major miners, which themselves indicate the strong support of shareholders for further investment and possible provision of additional capital if required. We will look at market capital values a little later in comparing steel companies to others.

Other resources

There will also need to be capital deployed for coking coal and other reductants, and for alloying materials. I have taken no account of these items as they are much less in total capital requirements than iron ore and add nothing to the discussion.

Can steel be funded?

This is a much more complex question. I have looked at a very global and macro level, so far, and the performance of steel is very poor. The average EBIT margins, shown in Chapter 1, of 5.3% are only a fraction of those for iron ore. To look at this differently, I will present a real example of the economics of an actual steel plant proposal.

A greenfield case

The case is that of a greenfield plant, to be located in India and promoted by an international steel group who had excellent credentials as a plant operator. It was conceptualised as an integrated plant, using local and imported purchased raw materials delivered to the factory gate, so there was no need for capital for mines and external infrastructure, although power and water-treatment plants for onsite use were required. The technology would all be proven and established: coke, sinter, blast furnaces and BOFs etc. The product mix was to be 50/50 between hot rolled bars and sections and hot rolled pickled and oiled coil. For both these products, there was a strong and growing local demand so the ramp up to full production was not seen as constrained by demand, only by the practicalities of commissioning. Total steelmaking capacity was for 12Mt p.a. The Indian market had been growing at about 8% p.a.. Equity funding was to be from the balance sheet of the parent which was strong and soundly based, mostly from international sources. Debt in the first instance was to be at the corporate level, so guaranteed by the parent with a best in class credit rating. Given the technology, political environment and the credibility of the promoter and operator, risks were perceived as modest.

A full feasibility study was undertaken by an international, widely experienced consulting firm as the promoter was not deeply experienced in new-build, greenfield projects. Exhibit 8.1 shows the IRRs achieved by the project and the sensitivity of the IRR to variations in a number of key elements in the economics. The underlying IRR was 11%. This was calculated at pre-tax and un-escalated for any inflation. The IRR is the internal rate of return. This is the return having funded the project assuming the company's weighted average cost of capital. It also takes into account the cash flow funding of the project, with appropriate working capital needs, the timing of construction and the buildup of market penetration with associated payment terms etc.. As we all know the business cycle is critically important for steel, and the cycle was taken into account, with the assumption being that the plant began production at the midpoint of the cycle.

The IRR was inadequate, both in absolute and relative terms. In absolute terms the return has to be set against a WACC of around 8%. It would also need to be taxed. To this has to be added the element of uncertainty and risk specific to the project. The WACC incorporates the risk profile of the company's established businesses, spread around different political environments, mostly low risk mature economies, reflecting the current locus of steel production and consumption. A new project of this nature has risks specific to itself, not least the execution risk - that is the risk that the project will not be delivered on time, to specification, in this geography with minimal cost overrun. The project cost of capital was, therefore, higher than the corporate cost and after adjustment the project returned nothing. The project included a capital cost contingency of 15%.

EXHIBIT 8.1: WHAT RETURNS CAN A GREENFIELD STEEL PLANT EXPECT AND WHAT MAKES A DIFFERENCE TO THESE RETURNS?

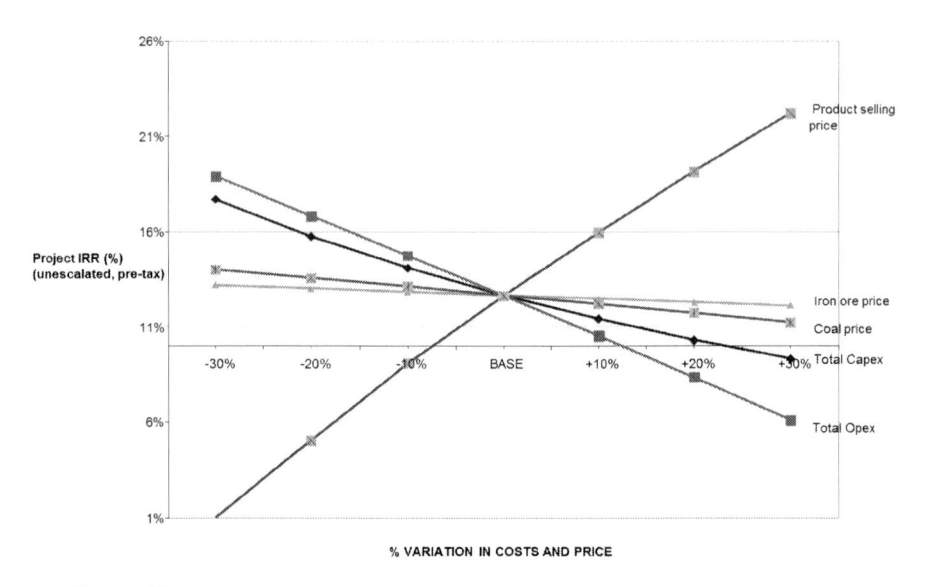

Source: Hatch

In addition, shareholders need a return and the company is striving to improve its returns to its shareholders and enhance its stock market profile and rating. In mining and metals, with private sector companies, the expected rate of return for projects is seldom below 15% - between that and 20% is the desirable range. This project was well below that target. In relative terms all projects are competing internally for the allocation not just of capital, but also of scarce, talented management time and attention. Other projects had a better return and lower risk profile. These were overwhelmingly brownfield projects offering incremental expansion and lower capital cost per tonne.

Whilst this was disappointing, the sensitivity analysis was revealing. The most obvious elements of the project to look at are the operating costs and the capital cost. Given that the technology was established and fundamental alternatives did not exist, then the capital reduction involved possible alternative sourcing and the potential to reduce capex per tonne by building a larger plant. Neither of these approaches produced much in the way of benefit. The scale would only have leveraged the infrastructure, about 15% of the total capital, and the alternative sourcing would entail gains at the cost of higher risk. Operating cost was likewise, and somewhat surprisingly, not greatly sensitive. The plant had been designed for efficient use of labour and consumables so little savings could be made. India is a low labour-cost country and increases in efficiency in labour are modest in impact. The company had many assets in many countries and was well aware of global best practices.

On raw materials, again, the impacts were surprisingly small. In the case of iron ore, given the emphasis the steel industry currently puts on the challenges posed by raw material prices, the flat curve for this sensitivity, shown in the chart, was unexpected. On reflection, as we have seen elsewhere, when raw material costs vary so do prices and thus margins, so both ends of the economic equation need taking into account. Some caution must be applied also due to local circumstances. The region where the plant was to be built had abundant iron ore reserves and operating mines. The delivered price to the plant took into account that the material would not be part of the seaborne trade and so would not carry costs for transport to a sea port, intercontinental deep sea costs and associated local transport costs. Thus the price was inherently lower than the seaborne benchmark price. Also as the ore was for domestic use, the tax regime would be lower. The plant did not benefit from owned iron ore, but it definitely did benefit from lower cost ore compared to steel producers dependent on the international seaborne market. This made the original IRR look even more anaemic and unattractive – if international ore prices had been used the IRR would have deteriorated.

The only variable that could make a substantial difference to the IRRs was selling prices or, rather, enhanced margins from higher prices assuming the benefit was retained by the producer. This study was conducted at a time when the market did not look very different than it does today, around early 2014. Selling prices on the spot Asian market were at approximately $700 /t for hot rolled coil, standard grade products; iron ore prices were at $110 /t, some $20 cheaper than when I am writing this; coal prices were about the same. So, the net effect of these elements was to provide slightly higher margins than are available today. The slope of the line for selling prices on the chart is dramatic. A 30% increase in margins, taking selling prices from $700 to $910, raises the IRR from 11% to 20%. At that level, the project would go ahead. At present, it has not been implemented.

Here, we see the downside of the long process of radical improvements in efficiency that steel has achieved. There is little that the industry can do with capital and operating costs to achieve higher returns; they have already reached a high plateau. Of course radical new technologies might change this, but these are not available widely today and are likely to be copied over time; as they always are. Given the independence of the mining sector in general, steel producers have little leverage on these elements. The market holds the secret to enhanced returns but, sad to say, it is the element in the economic equation which too often gets the least attention. The key is to raise the margin available to the steel company and to retain this enhancement. In the next chapter, I shall address this directly and point to how this can be done.

The capital markets and steel

This case example of low returns on a new plant reflects the low historical returns as a whole. We saw in a previous chapter that the EBIT return for the industry for the last 30 years, including the years of plenty between 2003 and 2007, was 5.3%; compare this with Rio Tinto's iron ore business in 2013 which was 38%. The 5.3% is required to pay tax, to pay interest and to offer shareholders a return through dividends. Interest is unlikely to be less than 2% of turnover, tax is unlikely to be less than 25% on EBT leaving perhaps 2.5% of revenues for shareholders and new investment. The revenues of the steel industry are approximately $150bn ($1000 /t on 1.5bnt). 2.5% of this is $33.75bn whilst the annual growth capital need was seen to be $59bn.

Capital markets appreciate this underperformance which provides no reason for them to be willing to provide new capital for expansion. The market capitalisation of ArcelorMittal is $20.5bn; that of Nucor is $15.3bn. These are two major and better performing steel companies. Their combined shipments were 108Mt in 2013. Taking that as a proportion of global production and valuing the total at their average value would provide a total capitalisation of $497bn. Yet these are the higher performing steel companies. I doubt if the total industry could be valued at more than $250bn. Exxon is valued at $394bn and Rio Tinto at $108bn. This is an industry requiring $59bn of new capital every year!

The industry as it performs and is structured today is incapable of funding the required growth out of internally generated profit or from capital markets. As the CEO of Gerdau asked his New York audience: "How to think outside the box?...How to reinvent ourselves?...We cannot continue to do the things we have been doing."

But….we are getting cheaper iron ore and that will solve the problem!

There is a view, becoming common in the industry and financial community, that we are about to experience a glut of iron ore and that this will lead to a substantial decline in the price, probably a structural decline such that the long-term price might be as low as $80 or $90 /t for the benchmark grade. Such a decline would potentially reduce the cost of iron by $80 and provide the necessary uplift in EBITDA and suddenly the steel sector would be free of its chains.

This will not happen. Putting aside the predilection of the steel producers to give away added margin to the market, there are more fundamental reasons to doubt this happy scenario. The cost curve for ore shows that the marginal tonne today is close to the CFR China price. It is a tonne in China. Chinese costs are rising inexorably and capacity will close over the coming years. This closure could be quickened if the renmimbi hardens against the dollar. Iron ore is priced in dollars and so seaborne ore would become cheaper to Chinese steelmakers. At the same time, all mining costs are rising, not just through inflation but through poorer grades and longer and more complex logistics.

The history of mine expansion forecasts is that they are always missed on the downside. Projects take longer to bring in than the junior entrepreneurial companies predict. Something unexpected always happens. But what if the capacity is coming in via the big three or four miners? This capacity will be low or middle cost and will mean that the marginal cost will decline and, with it, the price. This is to misunderstand the nature of iron ore market dynamics. With most services and products, a missed sale is a loss of a sale. Airline seats are lost when the plane takes off empty. Even car assembly capacity is partially lost if a sale is not made. The capacity can be used another day but there are still maintenance costs to pay. A lost iron ore sale is merely a delayed sale. Leaving ore in the ground does not mean it goes away – rather it might be beneficial as the price tomorrow might be higher than today: this is the nature of depleting assets. Agricultural commodities deteriorate and revenue is lost never to be recovered. With manufacturing capacity such as steel mills, when they are idled, the capacity is still depreciating and generating a loss. With iron ore, only the fixed costs are lost.

There is very little reason to pursue capacity utilisation in commodity mining and indeed there is much to be gained by keeping high-cost marginal producers in business to keep prices high. If I can produce at $50 /t and to do so would eliminate a producer at $120 /t and make one at $100 /t the marginal producer, why would I do so? The consequence might be to bring the price down for all shipments to $100 and the loss for me would massively outweigh the gain from the added volume. I would prefer to leave the ore in the ground to sell on another day.

Bearing all these factors in mind, it is impossible to see long-term iron ore prices lower than today (about $120-130) and very easy to see them rising steadily for the foreseeable future.

The crisis has a solution

Of course there is always recourse to governments for funds and in the last resort the state can fund anything – it can always print money. But to allow another cycle of state funding would be a disaster for the steel sector. The industry does recognise how deleterious the state is to its health. If the growth is to be funded by internally generated funds or new private capital, then, the industry has to generate increased EBIT. All that is required is about a 3-4 % increase. It is certainly less than double digits of EBITDA. I shall show how this can be done and how it is within the steel industry's ability and control to do it. Help is at hand and it is self-help. The key is customer service.

CHAPTER NINE

Solving the funding crisis: Delivering service

> *"Consumption is the sole end and purpose of production; and the interest of the producer should be attended to only so far as it promotes the interest of the consumer."* Adam Smith

Mature economies become service industry dominated

It is a truism well accepted that manufacturing is in decline in the UK economy, which is parallel to other advanced economies. Manufacturing now represents approximately 10-11% of the UK GDP, a decline from nearly 38% in 1970. There is a contrary trend such that the contribution of manufacturing to wealth has been rising: from £80bn in 1959 to £160bn today, measured in Gross Value Added. The underlying reason for the contrary trend is that productivity has grown quite strongly. This pattern of relative proportional decline but increased wealth contribution is common across all advanced economies. Measured in employment terms, all major economies have shown constant declines in the share of employment from manufacturing industry. This is true even in Japan which is seen as particularly strong in this area; here the proportion has fallen from 23%, in 1970, to 18%. In Germany the fall has been from 32% to 22%.

A parallel to this trend is the steady change in job specifications of employees in manufacturing companies. In the UK manufacturing sector in 1994, 55% of jobs were categorised as production. The remaining jobs were sales and marketing, services (both trades and professional), logistics and distribution, and research and development. By 2006 only 50% were in production.

Perhaps it comes as a surprise to realise that even China is losing manufacturing jobs; though it is still in a relatively early stage of development. It has seen a loss of several million jobs as inefficient state-owned enterprises have declined, to be replaced by much more efficient private sector enterprises. Of course, China has a demographic time bomb due to the single child policy. In early 2014 Beijing revealed that the country's working population has begun to shrink, much sooner than expected. It will soon go into precipitous decline. The decline of manufacturing seems set in stone for economies as they reach good levels of GDP.

This is not an economic catastrophe as service activities take over as growth engines. Indeed, the decline in manufacturing can be misunderstood, as the outsourcing of service activities into separate service businesses moves jobs and economic production between categories but does not change any reality. There should be no great surprise as people develop new tastes and requirements as wealth grows. They desire travel, holidays, more ease and comfort, all of which require service activities.

Even products become services

There is something else taking place here which is less commented upon but is of the greatest significance for business models in general and for steel in particular. Manufacturing and service businesses are increasingly merging and losing differentiation. There are numerous examples of this.

Rolls Royce does not make most of its money from jet engines as stand-alone products nor does it "sell" engines. It sells a service of engine performance. Airlines buy a predetermined performance in terms of fuel, time in service and time between servicing. Rolls Royce makes most of its money from the service and maintenance activity which follows from the initial sale. The jet engine business follows a service business model. This however is still classified as a manufacturing industry.

As economic development spreads, products become more complex and new technologies emerge at increasing speed, intellectual property and knowledge-driven businesses will become the norm. The integration of value and supply chains across the world will require very high service levels to achieve the efficiency and performance needed by more knowledgeable purchasers and end consumers. One aspect of the internet is that it provides any purchaser with the capacity to access information on all potential suppliers and compare prices and functional characteristics as never before. This access to knowledge is destroying traditional sources of competitive advantage. Imperfect knowledge among purchasers, which being an inefficiency is a cost, has been a source of success for products and businesses. It has made market share of pre-eminent importance: from the provision of availability, the control of physical channels of distribution and the capacity for advertising. Just as the internet and related innovations destroy distance, they also destroy traditional barriers to competition. The most conspicuous example is Amazon which has virtually eliminated traditional book distribution.

This book is being self-published. I have no need of a traditional publisher as I can utilise my own electronic database of contacts to access the market of potential buyers. I don't need a publisher's credibility to access reviewers and traditional purveyors of their work to gain a market.

The provision of high service levels and extended products packaged with service elements, such as in the case of Rolls Royce, will be required in all business models which achieve and maintain competitive advantage. This will be reinforced by the continued growth of mass customisation. This enables products to be specified to meet individual customer needs in real time. For example, the multiplicity of variables which characterise a specific automobile will be chosen by the customer and made for him. Products, such as cars, will transform from products into services - in fact, they have already started this journey.

By 2050 will any, except a small minority, of cars be bought anymore? The function of on-demand reliable personalised transport is the desirable part of a car. As cars converge in their characteristics, including their styling, what is the purpose of owning one? There may have originally been an economic reason for ownership – it was cheaper than hiring, especially when car rental outlets were few – but the industry has matured. I need to get transported regularly from one place to another. I have little concern for how this is done and certainly I see little value in owning the means I use to arrive at my destination.

When cars first became available before World War I, they were luxury items which replaced horses and carriages for the well-off. Then, owners were often driven by chauffeurs - the owner bought a service. By 2050 or even well before, we will come full circle and motorised personal transport will be overwhelmingly provided as a service through rental or car clubs – a rapidly expanding sector of the market – rather than personal chauffeurs. There are still cars with prestige and style appeal, from which owners derive a pleasure through ownership: Ferraris, Bentleys, Porsches, but these are small minorities of vehicles.

There is now developed and ready for commercial testing, a system for computer driven cars. No human intervention will be required. The consequences of this will be that it will be possible commercially to call up a vehicle of whatever specification is required, on demand, to take you from A to B. These vehicles will be driven at optimal speed and safely. They will be able to drive much closer together than current vehicles driven by humans and so the capacity of roads will be radically increased.

Just like jet engines their performance will be able to be monitored in real time and any problems corrected between uses. Using a commercial rental organisation will be substantially superior in service to owning a car. It is time to buy car rental company shares!

This service revolution will spread along and throughout the value chains of the economy. It is relatively easy to imagine that customer-facing industries and their products will transform into services. But in fact all industries finish up as customer-facing. Eventually it is a customer who buys the product or service. Thus, all stages along the value chain will need to respond with total service performance and provision. If they don't, then the end product or service producer will suffer some deterioration in costs, quality and delivery which will be competitively disadvantageous. Over the last 30 years the Japanese have shown European and American industry the value of JIT, Kanban and lean manufacturing principles. These principles are thought of as having cost implications but they also have service implications. They will become dominant in all industrial value chains over the next two decades. This has profound consequences for steel which are nothing but positive.

How does steel perform on service?

When we buy a car, we expect it to be drivable out of the garage. It needs to have a wealth of features: how would we feel if it only had three wheels? What would we do if our mobile phone service failed on every other call? What if, when we went to the theatre, having booked our tickets three months before, we discovered someone else sitting in our seat? Even worse would be if, when taking a flight, we were told to expect only 90% of flights to arrive? This last example could be life-threatening! The purpose of any industry is to increase the wealth of society. A key element of that is service. We expect to receive good service: the right product, in the right quantity, in the right condition, at the right time to the right place. Certainly, we would not spend long thinking about changing suppliers as long as alternatives were available.

This is in the nature of Anglo-Saxon capitalism. Soviet industry was notorious for poor service – they had nothing to fear from dissatisfied customers. Industries which fail on service, systematically and consistently, will go out of business and be replaced. Steel does not experience this: the ubiquity and utility of the product and the systemic failure of all producers protects them from this self-correcting process. But poor service has close to catastrophic consequences for the industry. Putting this right will be a key element of transforming the industry to make it consistently financially successful and ensure its future.

EXHIBIT 9.1: CAR WITH 3 WHEELS

Every picture tells a story. The one above, Exhibit 9.1, was used for a long time as the introduction to a presentation. The presenter was the Managing Director of a very large steel customer. The audience was the executive committee of a very large European steel producer. The message was clear and simple – this is what I have to deal with when I order steel from you. The expectation was for no better than 75% delivery service. By service is meant delivery of the ordered quantity, in the specified grade, to the correct location, at the specified time;

commonly referred to as OTIF (on time in full). The three wheels indicated a 75% performance level. It was worse than that, in fact. The customer was, and still is, the largest single customer for this producer, enough surely to guarantee a high service level, and maybe relative to other customers this might have been the case. Also, the customer was wholly owned by the producer – it was the producer's own service and distribution business.

This experience is not unique: here are some real-life examples from email traffic between customers and suppliers. Let a major customer speak for themselves in their own words:

1. An order for 100t of universal columns. 72t sent on 26/10/12. 20t sent on 23/11/12. 8t still outstanding at 04/04/13.
2. An order for 100t of merchant bars. 76t sent on 26/11/12. 16t sent on 02/04/13. Remainder outstanding.
3. An order for sections of 50t. 40t sent on 29/10/12. 3t sent on 26/11/12. The supplier arbitrarily cancelled the outstanding 7t but failed to inform the customer.

As the company that provided these examples said to me; "There are many examples every month along the same lines. In addition, our largest supplier of long products often ignores what we request and sends a random selection of sizes and specifications"

No business should allow this to pass. But this level of service is accepted as a normal circumstance. Please examine the photo in Exhibit 9.2, which has been doctored only to the extent of hiding the name of the culprit, to protect the guilty. This is a photograph taken in 2010 at the gate of a major steel works. Again the target for service is defined as above. Imagine that your mobile telephone service provider aimed for a less than 70% performance in connecting your calls? You would find this unacceptable. The actual service level is astonishing. Yet steel companies can achieve high service levels when they are absolutely in a position where customers are strong enough to demand it; but they do struggle to achieve what the customer would like.

EXHIBIT 9.2: PERFORMANCE RECORD FOR AN ACTUAL STEEL MILL

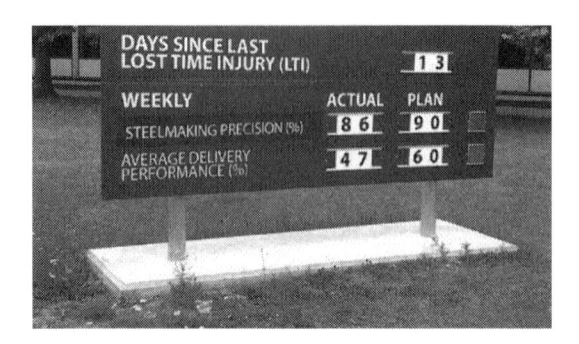

Source: Author's own photo

The packaging industry is one of the most highly competitive in the world. Alternative packaging materials are easily available and innovation is continuous: plastics, glass, aluminium, paper and cardboard. Tin-coated steel, tinplate, has been under attack and in retreat for generations. This product is very sophisticated and requires tightly controlled metallurgy and close tolerance coating. The value added by the tin can producers is low and they need to deliver cans to the fillers just in time, to minimise inventory. They are delivering to packagers who are canning time-sensitive food and drink products and must deliver to tight schedules to distributors and retailers. The can producers must meet in excess of 95% delivery performance. A continuous complaint from them is that they cannot get better than mid-70% delivery performance from the steel producers. Still, such delivery performance is much better than the average.

Steel can achieve high service levels

The greatest improvement in service levels, compared to 20 years ago, has been in supply to the automotive industry. Automotive manufacturing and especially assembly is highly competitive. Standards of manufacturing performance have been revolutionised by Japanese producers. They have focused on lean manufacturing and especially on Just in Time (JIT) delivery. The steel suppliers have had to meet these requirements or exit the supply chain. So, steel can deliver good service. What the industry needs to do is to provide this level of service to smaller and less powerful customers because it is in their own interests.

In specific segments, service can be the key aspect of the business. In Oil Country Tubular Goods (OCTG), Tenaris created a revolution by focusing on this specific sub-segment of pipe and tube production and realising that for the customer, service was what counted. OCTG products had been originally just another part of most seamless tube mills order books. The mills were nationally owned, often part of large integrated steel mills and groups. The demand for these products grew with the oil and gas industry, but fairly modestly as the technical demands on the product were low whilst wells were shallow and environments were relatively benign: for example Texas or Saudi Arabia rather than the Arctic or the Gulf of Mexico.

Following the price rises of the 1970s and as developing markets became more important, rising oil demand forced development of more challenging wells in more remote locations. OCTG products became more sophisticated, but also the cost of failure of a tube in drilling or production, rose ever higher. A drill rig or production platform costs millions a month to operate and every hour is valuable. The cost of a tube is trivial in this situation; to the driller or producer, service; as availability and guaranteed performance, is almost priceless; certainly much more valuable than the cost of production of a tube which might be $1,500 /t. Tenaris saw these developments and built a global business through acquisition of tubing subsidiaries in several countries, then added global distribution and in-depth technical support to service the oil and gas drillers.

So good service can be and is delivered – but mostly it is not. Whilst the cost to the average widget-maker is not as high as it is to drillers of oil wells, it is still substantial and represents a major lost margin opportunity for the steel companies. Solving this challenge will go a long way to achieving better financial performance. It is like a missing piece in a jigsaw.

The cost of poor service delivery

On the whole, this is hard to fix to a high degree of accuracy. These costs are normally hidden in general expenditures and not isolated in company management accounts. For a customer, the response to poor service can take a number of forms, often several: over-ordering from a supplier, order chasing, using multiple suppliers, holding excessive stock in inventories, and using service centres at higher prices than direct mill deliveries.

We need to consider again the position of our widget manufacturer and conduct another thought experiment. For her, the cost she needs to avoid is a lack of good service to his customer as this could threaten her business's existence. The example I will use is a widget company having a turnover of $50M and an EBITDA of 8%, holding 3 months inventory of steel and where steel is 50% of the total cost of goods sold. This is not an untypical medium-sized manufacturer in any economy in the world. There are a number of elements of cost which can be identified as arising from poor service.

1. If the 3 month's inventory, having a total value of $6.25M, could be reduced by 2 months by more reliable supply, the company would save nearly $2.08M in working capital. At a cost of finance of an estimated 10% that is $208k p.a., equivalent to nearly 1% of the price of the annual steel purchase.

2. Much management time and expense will go on progress chasing, warehouse space has to be overprovided and the inventory managed. This again can be over 1% of purchased cost.
3. Steel is a product sensitive to handing and damage, especially coil product. This again can amount to 1% of costs. Half of this can be allocated to holding excess inventory.
4. Sourcing from multiple suppliers is a typical risk mitigation strategy. This is hard to estimate but a conservative view would be that this must be worth at least as much as reduced inventory, so another 1% of steel costs.
5. Customers can either buy direct from mills or go via distributors or service centres. Should a customer go to distributors for 25% of her supply to compensate for, or insure against, poor delivery from the mills, that will add 20-25% to the cost of that supply. This is 25% on $6.25M of steel, or $1.25M p.a.; equivalent to 5% of the total cost of steel bought.
6. A further cost which is indeterminate but substantial is that of production disruption. If the widget manufacturer disappoints his customers the consequences can be very unfortunate so there is a bias to risk-mitigation. One way of handing this is to hold stocks of finished goods for delivery to customers in the hope that any disruption to production will be resolved before the excess stocks are exhausted. One month's finished goods supply is worth $4M; again, at 10% cost of capital, this is $400k, or about 1.5% of the value of steel purchased.

By these six items alone, it is possible to see that poor service adds over 10% to the costs of the steel purchased by the customer. If this potential saving were shared between customer and supplier, then the steel company would enhance its EBITDA margin by over 5%; this alone would take it to the financial success required according to McKinsey. However there are sectors where such improvements cannot be achieved such as automotive sheet products. So the increased margin applies only to a majority of shipments not all. There are other costs which cannot be quantified, perhaps the most important being the disruption caused by poor quality product. This obviously can lead to direct disruption in production lines within the works but it has all sorts of knock-on effects as well, such as delayed service to end customers.

The steel company also pays for poor service

Service improvement would have other benefits. Many of the costs to the customer of poor service are matched by costs to the steel company. A few examples of orders under-delivered and delivered at different times were provided earlier in this chapter. The disruption of failed or incomplete deliveries, the need to disrupt or leave excessive flexibility for emergencies in rolling programs, the over-rolling which leaves products without customers, and a dozen other costs are unnecessary with high service performance. All these costs are eroding the margins for the steel company.

I have ignored the cost of poor product quality, when the product does not meet its technical specification. Steel companies have been very good at tackling this problem and whilst it still exists I have chosen for this purpose to ignore the costs of this. I think I have demonstrated enough of the value enhancement for steel suppliers and customers without examining product quality. What I will not ignore is the opportunity for steel companies to enhance service through mitigating price risk for their customers.

Provide price risk management to your customers

In the next chapter I will examine the objections voiced to price risk hedging mechanisms (PRHM) in the steel sector. As a set of financial tools the common term for reference is PRM (price risk management). I regard these tools as fundamental to achieving financial success and adequate returns on capital for steel companies. But these tools also offer a major opportunity from a marketing perspective. The customers suffer from risk exposure from the volatility in steel prices even more than producers. Steel represents as large a percentage of their cost structures as raw materials do for steel producers. Given the small size of the average steel buyer and the commensurate limited access to capital of these companies, their exposure to prices is even more threatening than for the suppliers. Most steel buyers are small privately owned firms which are dependent on local banks and short term loans such as overdrafts for working capital. It is traditionally these enterprises which are worst placed in a downturn. They have few options for borrowing if facilities are withdrawn at short notice and no negotiating power with their banks.

As steel companies take to using PRHMs they will have the capability to offer such tools to their customers. The steel company's size will enable them to develop deep skills, and their large network and base of customers will enable them to package up risk and negotiate good terms with financial intermediaries so as to obtain the best terms for financial derivatives with the lowest costs. This is a once-in-a-generation opportunity to change the marketing mix and offer enhanced service to customers. Price risk management services will provide direct advantages to the steel company, but used as part of the marketing mix their benefit to the customers will be even more important. It will provide a direct profit opportunity through the sale of the service.

The greatest benefit will come through the long-term transformation of the market dynamics between customer and supplier. Today steel companies have reasonably good relations with only a minority of customers such as automotive manufacturers. These, though, show the benefit of good service: the relations are stable and involve mutual commitment as to long-term supply. If an enhanced service offer spreads across sectors it will solidify the supplier and customer relationship and reduce supplier switching. Improved loyalty will reduce the risk of volume volatility in downturns as customers will have a reduced temptation to switch. There will be improved bi-lateral production planning. This, complemented by PRHMs as a service offer, will make economic cycle volatility much easier to manage along the supply chain. In addition steel companies seeking to "dump" product and cause a downward price spiral will be less able to do so. The benefits of improved stability in the steel market cannot be over-emphasised.

What holds back higher performance?

This chapter has focused on service to customers. I have shown that poor service can cost a customer 10%+ of the steel purchase price. This cost is replicated in additional costs to the steel company and the missed margin opportunity from providing services such as PRHMs to customers. Nowhere else is there a 20% margin enhancement opportunity to steel companies. The constraint to achieving improvement is cultural. In any managerial system, there are a set of complex objectives: capacity utilisation, cost saving, asset optimisation, sales price enhancement, product development, expansion, rationalisation etc. In my experience, there are only rare exceptions of companies prioritising service as top of the objectives and management agenda. Indeed, it is not unreasonable to assert that for many steel companies service does not appear among the top five objectives. Furthermore, there is a tendency to fail to measure service accurately and so to pretend that service levels are higher than they really are. Perhaps if senior executives of steel companies spent more time visiting customers, especially the forgotten widget manufacturers, it would have a beneficial effect.

To start the revolution in service and the transformation in performance requires a commitment to service as the primary objective. The required improvements will not happen until this happens. It will take a major cultural shift as the industry is adept at understanding and articulating all the reasons why high service performance is difficult, even impossible: large inflexible units of capacity; high fixed costs requiring high utilisation; complex product mixes; unscheduled and unpredictable interruptions to production; complex multiple stage manufacturing processes; poor returns requiring high asset utilisation levels. It is time to examine critically all these objections as the prize for overcoming them is immense and the prize will go to those who achieve it early. It should be unacceptable under any circumstances for customers to receive less than 95% service performance.

CHAPTER TEN

Finding contentment: Managing volatility

> *"It isn't that they can't see the solution. It is that they can't see the problem."* G K Chesterton

Man is born to uncertainty

Uncertainty comes with us at birth; there is still a significant chance of infant mortality even in countries with excellent health systems. Our genes are never predictable and our skills and capabilities often surprise ourselves and others. The vicissitudes of life are multifarious and risk, uncertainty and chance follow us everywhere. Hence we have many phrases and sayings which capture aspects of uncertainty: "don't count your chickens before they are hatched", "it is better to be born lucky than rich", and so on. We often voice discontent with this circumstance but that is misplaced; uncertainty adds greatly to the joys of life. We might express a desire for our favourite football team to win every game but we would find the outcome quickly bored us. So we cannot escape risk and its concomitant, various forms of misfortune, but we can often mitigate the consequences.

Insurance

Two years ago I experienced extreme heart failure symptoms. One of the four valves in my heart had simply disintegrated or, rather, the fine short straps which hold the valve together had broken. A heart valve is like a tiny parachute. This condition became very serious, very quickly. I received good treatment at a fine London National Health Service (NHS) hospital, but if I had allowed them to operate on me they would, as a matter of policy, have removed the troubled valve and replaced it with titanium or a pig's valve. The result would have worked adequately but would have meant permanent medication and a further replacement every 10 years. These consequences would have reduced my life expectancy. I had private medical insurance. This proved fortunate. My excellent GP found a cardiac consultant and she recommended the most superb surgeon. He was a northern Italian – no humour but great skills. The idea of using a valve from one of my own pigs did not amuse. The result was a repair at great expense but much superior to a replacement as it does not require ongoing medication and should now be permanent.

There is a theory of industrial development which emphasises clusters of like skills as being self-reinforcing. This seems to be true of Northern Italy. It has for centuries been a world centre, if not the world centre, for precision engineering from Antonio Stradivarius, through Enzo Ferrari, to my consultant; for what is surgery if not precision engineering? He was able to repair the valve. This precision skill base and industrial characteristic probably dates from the Renaissance, for the explosion in the quality and complexity of painting, sculpture and building which occurred then was in essence craft skill. Painting is surely precision engineering using oil or tempura and wood or canvas as media, but imbued with communicable feeling. The repair of my heart meant no medication, no further 10-year replacements, but repair is more expensive than replacement and so the NHS does not fund repairs. The chances of my survival were improved and my life expectancy was extended – my heart has been reconditioned like a car engine – by insurance.

Insurance is a way of paying small amounts to mitigate a low-risk possibility which, if it occurs, has large-scale consequences. When many people take this route then the sum of all the small premiums covers the high cost of mitigation, either financial or otherwise. So we insure many things in our private lives: health, house, possessions, pets, cars etc. Although the cost of insurance involves a net loss for all the participants in the scheme, for the insurance company needs its costs covered and its shareholders rewarded, our aversion to risk and the consequences of unforeseen occurrences makes it worthwhile. This risk aversion is not irrational. If a house burns down not only would many people be unable to finance an alternative, they would find the distress of the event very painful and difficult; indeed they might find the stress caused them to have heart failure!

Companies will insure for similar reasons. Key man insurance provides the funds to pay for the search and recruitment of a replacement senior executive. It also pays for some of the disruption to the business. Insurance is taken out to cover various liabilities such as for negligence. Some very large companies will "self-insure", by which they avoid the insurance premium, and the costs entailed for the service. They prefer to rely on the saved premiums funding the inevitable occasional crystallisation of risk. For example, if they are very large with many factories then they will calculate the rebuilding of one can be funded from the saved premiums. They take the chance that two such events will not happen together.

Perhaps, the most ubiquitous and important of all insurances are pension funds. These are designed to cover the risk we run of reaching a stage when we cannot work but still live. How do we survive without a wage or salary? Of course some are lucky and have capital but the vast majority of people do not have such a safety net. So over the last century or so, pension funds have come to be the major source of saving for the provision of income after working life ends. This is a new phenomenon: in the UK, state pension funding only started in 1906. Pension funds generate capital to fund productive economic capacity which future generations – our children and grandchildren – will operate to produce income for the funder many years later.

Pension funds also prove Karl Marx's belief, that the workers would own the means of production and distribution, to have been correct. Communism in one of its fundamental economic predictions has arrived, as pension funds are mainly owned by workers and they own the majority of the capital listed on the world's stock exchanges. Marx may have been wrong in the institutional instrument by which worker ownership would emerge but he was right about its eventual occurrence.

EXHIBIT 10.1: IRON ORE FUTURES AND DERIVATIVES TRADING VOLUMES* (Mt)

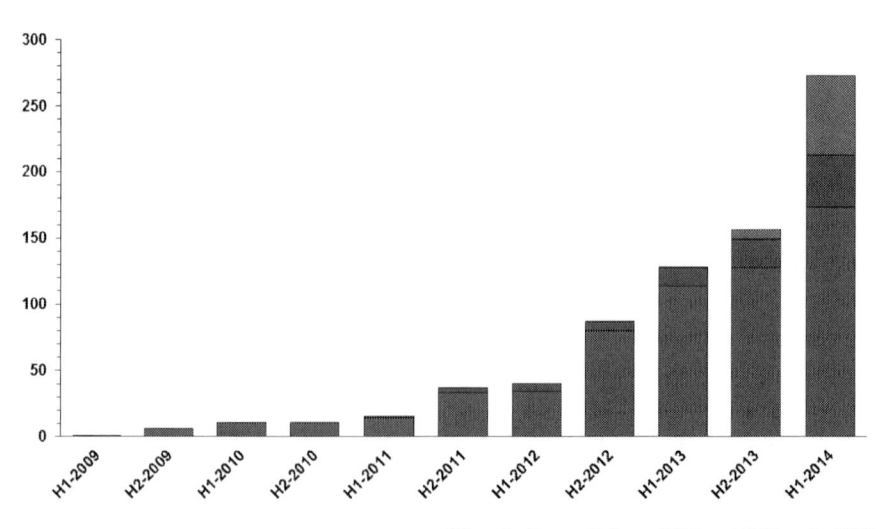

* Cleared by Singapore Exchange, CME Group, LCH.Clearnet and NOS

■ Swaps ■ Options ■ Futures

Source: The Steel Index (TSI)

Steel companies and insurance

Steel companies use insurance policies just as do other organisations: pension funds for executives, fire insurance, health insurance and all the other instruments available. The senior executives of steel companies do likewise for themselves and their families. This is just common sense. It is standard practice. The practices of forward and futures contracts are used by steel companies when it comes to consumable commodities such as energy, and financial instruments are readily available to achieve risk mitigation. The prices of oil and gas and electricity can be hedged by being bought forward actually or virtually through financial futures. Not all steel companies will necessarily do this but it is fair to say that it is a very common practice. Likewise, non-ferrous metals are subjects of well-established forwards and futures contracts, some, as we have seen, dating back to the 19th century, including those for copper and aluminium. I doubt there is any steel company which does not use hedging for its foreign exchange exposure.

This use of PRM tools also applies to some of the metals used by steel companies. Steel production consumes major portions of other metals' production. It uses over 50% of zinc, most nickel and chrome and manganese, large volumes of coking coal, and many minor metals used as alloying elements such as vanadium and molybdenum etc. Electric arc producers rely on scrap for the overwhelming majority of their feedstock. In some of these cases, futures or forward contracts exist; for example, in zinc and nickel, and other contracts are under development and consideration. Steel companies use these contracts to hedge, or manage, their risks. This is price risk insurance and does not differ in the slightest degree from other forms of insurance.

Recently, there have been dramatic changes in the pricing of iron ore. For decades, with the growth of the seaborne trade during the 1970s, 80s and 90s, ore was priced annually. Steel companies, therefore, knew the price for each year; it was fixed in an annual round of negotiations. The price was also low. In the last decade, this system has collapsed and prices are now set at spot, or a moving average of spot. Uncertainty rules the iron ore price. Consequently, iron ore futures contracts, and in parallel scrap contracts, are becoming increasingly common in their use by the steel producers and traders. Exhibit 10.1 provides the data to show this growth.

However, when it comes to the hedging of risk, or insuring for the consequences of risk, on steel products themselves, steel companies have been reluctant to recognise these possibilities. There is an apparent anomaly here. Steel companies will take out insurance on the housekeeping activities, health, pensions etc. They will hedge the price risk on significant elements of their cost structure such as alloys and energy. Although they have been slow to make use of the possibilities in iron ore - their critically important raw material whose price volatility is regularly cited as a major challenge for steel profitability - this is changing. The volumes of futures contracts in iron ore are rising rapidly. However, when it comes to their customers and the pricing of their own product, they are very reluctant to embrace change.

Insurance across the industrial value chain

Companies cannot insure directly against price volatility. But for commodity products, mitigation is available through forward and futures contracts. The price of oil is available into the future through the futures contracts on various exchanges, or in over the counter transactions. This has happened since the oil price shocks of the 1970s. Oil producers wish to lock in the price of their product in the future and the users wish to do the same so financial instruments arose to enable this to happen. This is not new. Since the 19th century, the London Metal Exchange (LME) has provided a forum for buyers and sellers of metal to buy and sell forward. For this to function, they created forward contracts. The origins of the LME lie in the emergence of new sources of raw material, specifically copper from Chile. This was required by

UK industry as local supplies ran out and became too expensive. Ships from Chile took several months to arrive and so forward contracts were created to cover this period and then later much longer timescales. They also created a network of storage facilities whereby someone who had bought forward and had no immediate use for the product when the due date came, could store the material and await a better time to use it or to sell on. The level of stocks in the LME warehouses indicated to users and traders the state of the market in terms of the balance of supply and demand and so they produced forward price curves. When stocks were high, then consumption was seen as lower than production, and the forward curves of prices showed a downward curve; and vice versa.

The forward curve then also created a mechanism to sell or buy against future production or consumption, so "locking-in" a price. If you were a copper wire drawer and had a clear committed demand for wire over the next 12 months from your customers, you could go to the LME and buy forward on the curve, so ensuring no price risk from your feedstock, and you could build that into your contracts for sales. The net result would be that, for a small fee to the trader and the LME, you avoided price risk. The wire drawer would have an insurance policy against the consequences of price changes.

For oil, there are limited third-party storage facilities and buyers and sellers must take and use or store at their own facilities. There are two standard quotations: West Texas Intermediate and Brent crude. The same dynamics occur for futures contracts in oil as for futures contracts in metals. The massive liquidity - a term used by financiers and traders to mean simply volume of activity in something - in oil and LME metals means that forward prices can be used for many years forward, certainly for five years in the case of LME metals. This is highly desirable for businesses with long-term lead times such as major construction contracts or even manufacturers with long planning cycles such as automotive assemblers. It also has major implications for financing of capital projects, enabling bankers to have a degree of security for loan repayments if commitments can be made to sell ahead of production at predetermined prices.

Aversion to change is not risk avoidance

Aversion to change is not of course an avoidance of risk; it is just a different risk! This reluctance to embrace change that has been shown to be useful elsewhere might be soundly based if the use of PRM tools was in itself risky or led directly to negative consequences in excess of the benefits derived.

The steel industry in public pronouncements is vigorously opposed to the use of financial price risk mitigation tools in the steel market. There are a number of arguments articulated as reasons for this. The four which I can identify as most common and perhaps most relevant are: that steel products are not commodities and have distinctly complex characteristics that make contracts impractical; that the presence of financial hedging instruments will lead to increased volatility; that they will lead to steel companies losing control of their markets and customers; and finally that the cost of such instruments will simply add costs without commensurate benefits. I shall address these in turn.

Is steel different... Does its complexity defy standardisation... Is that important

It is true that steel is not a commodity in that it comes in an almost infinite variety of grades, alloys, and many different forms: hot rolled strip, cold rolled strip, galvanised strip etc. But this is also true of oil and many other metals. Oil comes in different grades with many different chemical components. Aluminium is used in many different alloys and in as many forms as steel. However, in the case of aluminium, the LME specification of a particular purity is predominantly what the smelters make, and this is the metal quoted on the LME. Alloying is carried out later in re-melting and casting processes. In the case of steel, for technical and economic reasons, it is made directly in its alloy state. There is an intermediate product iron, pig iron, but this is alloyed immediately and in liquid condition. It exists only in small quantities as a traded and marketed product. There is no mass market steel grade which could be regarded as the equivalent of the LME aluminium grade. So steel is, to a degree, different and it does defy standardisation.

However, this difference is easily accommodated. Its irrelevance is written into all steel company price lists, which are available publicly in regions such as N. America and Europe where they are used for a very significant percentage of transactions. I have reproduced a portion of such a list, for hot rolled coil, in Exhibit 10.2. Standard qualities and forms are used as a base price point. This is now the subject of a public spot price listed in trade publications and collated by such as CRU and TSI for specific pricing locations. Then extras or premiums are added for variations, however complex. Gauge, alloy, width, form etc. can all be accommodated in the pricing structure as seen in the chart. This is no different from the LME metals contract. Here a user buys a contract for forward purchase and the product specified is the aluminium equivalent of the standard base product in steel's spot price. The product he actually uses will be a variant on the standard, depending on his application, and various premiums will be added at the point and date of purchase. The user has effectively hedged the base portion, the majority, of the purchase price of his actual product but not the premiums.

The premiums will vary from producer to producer depending on their own cost structures and the preference they have, for market strategy reasons, for making one product rather than another. The underlying logic is the same. There is no inherent product reason why financial instruments such as forward or future contracts cannot be designed around the base steel quality and form.

EXHIBIT 10.2: ARCELORMITTAL EUROPE PRICE LIST EXTRAS HOT ROLLED COIL

Source: ArcelorMittal

If contracts can be thus designed, then the ability exists for steel companies to hedge out the price volatility risk of standard products, and the proportion of price which is constituted by the base price for even the most sophisticated products. Two questions follow: is there an acceptable base price index that all participants can trust and use? Is the base price significant enough to eliminate most of the price risk on the finished steel product? There are already various price indices for hot rolled products: the two important ones being hot rolled coil and hot rolled rebar. Steel producers use these base price indices in their pricing methodologies. They are known as spot prices and are referenced to specific locations, from which adjustments can be made for actual points of production and consumption through transport premiums. In the case of bars the additional cost associated with cold finishing or with alloying extras is only a small fraction of the hot rolled cost. For coil products, it is more significant but only a minority of cost. For a cold rolled strip of a non-standard gauge, the premium might total $200 /t, but the hot rolled base price today is at $650. So over 75% of the price risk could be hedged. A product could be ordered today for delivery in many months, mature and developed futures financial instrument markets would allow the buyer and seller to lock in 75% of the price as the order is finalised. Because the premium is specific to the individual steel producer there can be no way to develop instruments to hedge this potential risk.

Steel companies are exposed to volatility in price at both ends of the value chain. They buy iron ore, scrap and other commodities which have fundamentally changed in pricing over the last decade. Iron ore is now subject to spot prices whereas it used to be the subject of annual pricing contracts. The result of spot prices is that steel companies are exposed. In the case of iron ore, the use of futures is expanding rapidly. The Exhibit 10.1 shows the take-up of these contracts over the last few years. Maybe iron ore is a true commodity, one with a single predominant grade of ubiquitous use, so lacking the claimed complexity of finished steel products?

This is not the case. Iron ore is indeed more complex than steel. There is no body of ore which is the same as another when three factors are taken into account: iron (Fe) content, deleterious materials such as silica and phosphorous and physical form. They are all different. When they are mined, they generally go through some process of beneficiation, whether it is simple sorting, taking the non-ore out of the mined product, or more complex such as separating the silica as much as possible from the Fe. These processes result in a more uniform range of products but ones still subject to substantial variation. These variations are dealt with through the use of premiums against a base price – just like steel in company price lists. The most frequently used base is a 62% Fe fine ore delivered CFR to China. Additions are made for higher Fe, subtractions for lower Fe; additions are made for more economically attractive physical forms, lumps and pellets, and deductions for higher levels of deleterious materials.

There is a challenge to the use of forward contracts as opposed to futures. The difference is that forwards, as used by the LME, require the availability of terminal, physical, warehouses for delivery. Contracts are not just financial, automatically balanced and cancelled out with balancing payments at the due dates. The scale and value of metals such as copper, nickel and aluminium make the provision of warehousing feasible. With iron ore and steel, this is not possible. For example, steel production is 50 times that of aluminium and has a value per tonne of one third or less. For futures contracts, which are purely financial, this limitation does not apply.

The growth of use of iron ore contracts is enabling steel companies to hedge out price risk up stream although these are in a state of infancy as yet. In 10 years the market for iron ore financial contracts will have grown significantly.

Fundamentally, there is no particular complexity in steel products which should inhibit the growth of PRM tools in steel. There is no case to be made that the complexity of steel products in use is a barrier to the use of futures contracts.

Speculation and volatility

The existence of contracts of a purely financial nature allows for a market in these instruments to arise independent of the underlying product, such as steel or iron ore. Hence, speculation can occur. People or funds can buy and sell such instruments as a way of investing if they believe that the general market expectation is out of line with their own. The futures curve of prices is the sum of all market participants' expectations of future supply/demand balance developments. There are funds which take positions in the futures market as a part of their portfolio of investments, based on a careful calculation of risks and expectations of the likely movement in value of different investment classes.

If I have a fund of cash which I wish to deploy other than in a bank, I have a range of options. I can buy assets such as bonds, shares, an index tied to the movements of the stock market or a commodity. I can buy contracts for delivery of metal in the future or, indeed, I can sell such contracts. I can, in effect, take the risk of metal price fluctuations. Indeed, if no one is willing to take this risk, there is no means of selling it; and vice versa: hence, no ability to hedge. If I am a purely financial entity and have no production or use for production, I might be a gambler or an investor. But, this is true for all investment vehicles. If I buy a house, I am not just buying somewhere to live or to rent, I am buying ownership of the future change in value of the house, plus or minus, profit or loss. The same is true for stocks and shares and bonds or indeed for any deployment of cash in any asset. The same goes for commodity futures or forwards. Each of these embodies a degree of ignorance and hence gambling, and each a degree of intelligent assessment, hence, investment. Is the gambling element in futures contracts greater than that in steelmaking? The history of the last 30 years of steel makers' financial performance suggests that there is no greater gamble than steel shares. It might be more accurate to describe it as a one-way bet. There is a joke in the USA which asks – how do you make a million in the steel business? The answer is – you start with a billion. Sadly, this joke has too much reality behind it for comfort.

The answer to the anxiety about manipulation is liquidity and transparency. The larger the market and the greater the number of participants, the harder it is to manipulate the market. The more transparent the market and its transactions, the same applies. With a large and liquid market, investors will swamp speculators; if rationally motivated investors assess that the futures curve is poorly based – hence, subject to gambling - then they will correct that by making opposite investments and bringing the curve into line with their assessments. There is no way that accuracy can be guaranteed. Indeed, forecasting is a subject of scepticism throughout this book. Nobody accuses the oil futures market of being manipulated as it is just too big for that to happen. Steel and its related raw material market is, by value, second only to oil in size; let us hope financial instruments develop quickly to swamp even the possibility of manipulation.

But, does the existence of futures lead to greater volatility in prices? The charge seems to have some intuitive possibility if only because the market needs traders and they benefit by the margins they can make and take; these are more available the more the market moves, up or down. Hence, they can benefit from volatility and indeed require it - as, in fact, do all participants because if there was none, there would be no need for hedging. The only way to assess this is to look at the price movements for commodities which have and do not have futures opportunities. Preferably, this should be over long period of time. The Exhibit 10.3 shows the volatility of prices for nickel and oil against steel over the last 11 years; which incorporates a major economic cycle. It is hard to discern any difference in the volatility of the 3 products although only steel is not traded.

Control over markets

When steel executives mouth this concern I am tempted to ask "So you have control of your markets now?" No industry has control of its markets; if it did, it would be practicing a cartel and not fulfilling its economic function. Markets are, or should be, in control. It is the job of governments in capitalist societies to ensure this happens. There is little doubt that cartels and monopolistic practices have been seen in steel in the past; but those days are long gone. What steel executives and companies mean by invoking the fear of loss of control is that if financial instruments were to develop, then the metal grade they would use as the base for those instruments would be the one they were forced to make. This implies that customers are currently incorrectly specifying the grades they use. That they are in fact over specifying and wasting their resources by paying more than they need to for their steel. This hardly needs comment.

EXHIBIT 10.3: WEEKLY INDEXED PRICE (1ST JANUARY 2004 = 100 IN USD) FOR NICKEL (LME CASH PRICE), HRC (N. EUROPE EX WORKS) AND OIL (BREND SPOT FOB)

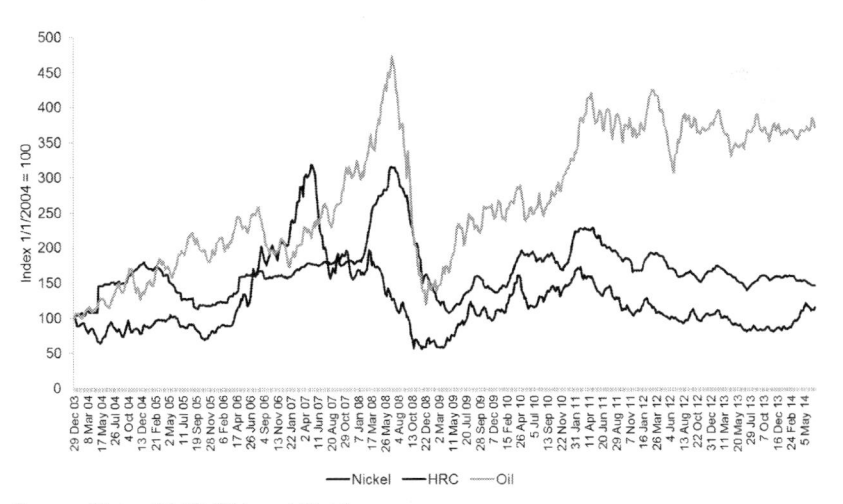

Source: Platts, LME, EIA and Hatch

Steel companies have been very successful in new grade innovation. Much emphasis in market strategy for steel has been placed on differentiation and the production of grades that have uniqueness and a higher value in use. These can be sold at higher prices and hopefully better margins as they deliver improved performance to the customer. For the automotive industry, steels have been developed with high strength and ultrahigh strength to give users the option to achieve the same or better functional performance with lighter weight. The fear is that if futures contracts specify a standard grade as the benchmark, then there will be an erosion of these differentiations and more steel will be made to the standard specification.

This is fundamentally to misunderstand the function of the financial market which works with a virtual product as much as an actual one. In the example of aluminium, the grade used by the LME does not need to exist as long as users of the LME benchmark know how to relate the actual grades they use to the benchmark. Just as with iron ore, the spot price could be a non-existent grade. It just happens to be one commonly available.

It also reveals a misunderstanding of the nature of product specification choice. A specific company such as BMW will choose its grades of steel on the basis of value in use in the context of a much bigger issue: the nature of the product it is to be used for. It will trade off cost against functional properties to make the optimum choice of material. This will apply to different steels as much as to other materials. It is a strange idea to think that its choice of steel grades would be at all influenced, never mind determined by, what the spot market may use as the reference grade of hot rolled coil. Customers such as BMW are sophisticated enough to take advantage of standard grades already if that suits their needs.

This choice is a technical and economic consideration completely immune to influence by financial instruments or markets. Indeed, if the negative economic effects of volatility of prices can be removed or reduced, then steel executives will increase their influence over their customers and reduce their desire to switch to other products which have achieved this result. The automotive companies are attracted to aluminium partly because the price risk can be hedged. After all, they make model and material decisions for five and ten-year periods when prices are bound to fluctuate substantially. As I shall show in the last chapter, the widespread use of PRM tools offers the opportunity for steel companies to transform the market for their products to the immense benefit of themselves. They are in danger of missing a monumental opportunity to break free from poor economic performance. PRM tools offer the prospect of advantageous transformation and effective price insurance.

Financial institutions will take all the profit

This objection is the easiest and simplest to remove. There is always a cost to any economic activity. The use of financial instruments is no different. The normal cost of taking out a futures contract in a developed market such as oil is one sixteenth of 1% of the value of the contract. In the short term the cost for steel will be larger as the market in their financial instruments is immature and lacks liquidity and competition. But in the longer term the rule of the sixteenth will apply. This can hardly be regarded as punitive. The cost of price security is a small proportion of the cost of volatility exposure.

In summary

In 2002 I led an exercise on behalf of the executive committee of the IISI (International Iron and Steel Institute – now the World Steel Association). This was to look at how forward contracts, those used on the LME, could operate in steel markets and what consequences, positive and negative, might flow from their operation. We conducted independent research and also interviewed all the members of the executive committee to elicit their views. Our conclusion was that there would be very large long-term benefits and my view remains the same. The views of the interviewees were deeply divided. The objections were very much the same as those I reviewed above. I believe these objections are as invalid now as they were then and the major blockage to the acceptance and rapid growth of futures (rather than forward) contracts remains fear and lack of understanding.

The answer to fear and misunderstanding in this area is the same as with all similar social conditions: it is education and mutual understanding. The mutuality is required between the steel executives and the professionals of the financial community. Futures contracts entail a lot of jargon and language which is incomprehensible to steel executives. If the financial community wants to promote the use of financial instruments in the industry, and it is to their benefit to do so, then that community has to carry the burden of explication and education. This has not yet been attempted in any serious or effective way. It will require people who are capable of understanding both worlds and translating between the two. The prize is worth the effort.

EXHIBIT 10.4: COST OF CAPITAL FOR DIFFERENT INDUSTRIES

Industry Name		Number of Firms	Cost of Equity/%	E/(D+E)/%	Cost of Debt/%	Tax Rate/%	After-tax Cost of Debt/%	D/(D+E)/%	Cost of Capital/%
Steel	2014	37	8.99	68.54	5.54	14.13	4.76	31.46	7.66
	2013	33	11.32	64.02	2.76	24.24	2.09	35.98	8.00
Utility (General)	2014	20	5.84	59.05	4.04	29.93	2.83	40.95	4.61
	2013	n/a	n/a	n/a	n/a	n/a	n/a	n/a	n/a
Utility (Water)	2014	20	6.78	63.33	5.04	14.52	4.31	36.67	5.87
	2013	11	4.61	57.74	2.76	31.45	1.89	42.26	3.46
Total Market	2014	7,766	8.07	57.38	6.04	10.32	5.42	46.62	6.94
	2013	6,177	8.53	69.97	3.26	14.93	2.77	30.03	6.80

Source: Reuters and Hatch

The biggest prize available to steel companies is the reduction in the cost or capital which applies to less volatile industries. There should be no surprise here; investors welcome reliable and stable earnings performance from their investments. As steel requires such large volumes of capital between now and at least 2050 any reduction in the cost of raising this capital is very welcome. Exhibit 10.4 shows the cost of equity for steel against utility companies and the whole equity market. Significant benefits await steel companies that reduce the volatility of their earnings; PHMs offer this prospect – why not seize it?

PRM tools are feasible for the steel sector through the value chain from raw materials to finished steel. They are just emerging in iron ore. The tools available will facilitate the management of the worst elements of price volatility which is such a damaging influence on profitability and financial viability. The objections to such instruments are based on misunderstandings about: how they work, the nature of speculation, the difference between product and financial markets and the cost of doing business. Furthermore, the steel companies should embrace and encourage the use of these instruments as they represent a once-in-a-generation opportunity to transform the workings of the market to their inestimable benefit.

CHAPTER ELEVEN

Technology

> *"Technology is just a tool. In terms of getting the kids to work together and motivating them, the teacher is the most important."* Bill Gates

Introduction

I am not a technologist, an engineer or a metallurgist so I cannot comment on the pros and cons of individual technologies or their likelihood of successful innovation and introduction from a technical perspective. Others are far more qualified than I to do this. I am an economist and can comment on the impact of industrial economics on the process of innovation. This is the subject of this chapter as it applies to the ferrous sector. As you may have gathered by now, this book is premised on the idea that economics drives all in the long run. It is not hard to identify where the biggest economic gains are to be found and thus where the incentive for success is greatest. In an earlier age, say of Bessemer, individuals working in near isolation were the generators of innovation. Their motivation could be variable and was often pure intellectual exploration and wonder. In today's age, the motors of innovation are large organisations able to fund and coordinate teams of multi-skilled experts. These institutions are motivated by economics and that alone; but individuals within these can be driven by internal political and career interests. The institutions are hindered by several syndromes such as "not invented here", "resistance to change" and the kind of sloth described below which often obscure this drive.

A Pyrrhic victory?

Technological change has been a continuous feature of the steel industry from its inception. We have touched on many aspects of this at many points in this book. The achievements have been praised as indeed they should be; they are enormous. The industry has shown exceptional ability to create new steel grades to meet new needs as well as developing and deploying new processes to utilise raw materials and to achieve great improvements in yields of these and of energy and labour.

Yet, the net result must be seen as disappointing in the extreme and depressing for the future. The industry has not achieved a financial performance which makes it self-sustaining. Without this all the technological wizardry and genius man can deploy is worthless as far as shareholders are concerned; although the customers in industry in general benefit. The way to financial success has been detailed in the previous chapters. These have been emphasised as they are critically important and under exploited and under emphasised by the current industry leaders and institutions. As these challenges in achieving and managing high service levels and managing volatility are met, and they will be met, then, perhaps, technology can be deployed for the benefit of the industry rather than just its customers.

But this is still an ambition very difficult to fulfill as only technological improvements that deliver competitive advantage will benefit companies. If technology is rapidly deployed throughout the industry then competition tends to result in lower prices and better products but without higher returns. This chapter explores what technology can contribute to the economics of the industry over the coming decades.

The pace of change

Before looking to specific technologies and areas of potential change, I wish to pause and examine the topic of the pace of change. There is a popular appeal in theses that argue for rapid and fundamental change. The promoters attract attention and the explosion of 24 hour news and of social media networks allow for scares and enthusiasms to spread virally. In the 1970s there was a popular book entitled "Future Shock", which argued that the speed of change was increasing rapidly and we would all be overcome with changes which emerged quickly and made planning essentially impossible. Forecasts that life is speeding up find favour with news channels but I find it hard to believe in these hypotheses of more rapid change.

Superficially, it appeals as digitalisation and computing increase the world's ability to accumulate knowledge and enormously speed up the dissemination of such knowledge. This naturally leads on to the thought that changes, resulting from such knowledge, will follow by also speeding up. There is the possibility that the cycle of invention, introduction, dissemination and obsolescence will become more rapid. This leap however assumes that only "knowledge" is important as a variable. What about the capacity of the humans using such knowledge to facilitate change and their ability to adapt to make changes successfully?

The first computer was designed and built during World War II to crack German ciphers; but it was based on development work done in the mid-19th century by Charles Babbage. The origins of the internet go back to packet-switching concepts in the late 1960s. Biotechnology can be seen as originating in antibiotics from before World War II. I would argue that all basic technological changes can be seen as arising two generations – 25 to 50 years - before they have transformational impacts on society or economics. The pace of change is slow as it is governed by human and societal factors. There is no secret reason for this sloth. The successful introduction and dissemination of innovation requires humans to adapt to new technologies and humans change slowly. It is now 50 years or more since social scientists noted the phenomenon of "resistance to change". People find it difficult and challenging to change even if it might be in their best economic or social interest to do so. Change just takes time and cannot be made more rapid.

Furthermore, major institutions such as governments or industrial organisations change predominantly by the replacement of elites, not by their elites changing their minds and their thinking. Pareto's observations about the circulation of elites are a permanent truism. This process is what gives democracy its competitive strength as a political system. As people, we find it difficult to give up our cherished ideas and beliefs; after all, those are what have been at the basis of our success in whatever we have done in our professional lives. They even form part of our very identities.

History is littered with cases of institutions that did not change, or changed but not fast enough, and finished on the scrap heap of history. Soviet communism is the most dramatic recent example but examples are all round us; not least here in Europe. How will history treat the Euro and the EU itself? The current "European empire" is likely to disappear just as all such previous attempts by Rome, Napoleon and Hitler, have disappeared.

In industry, examples litter the case studies of business schools. The liner shipping companies were overtaken by airlines and likewise the railways by the automobile and airlines. Kodak is no more, eclipsed by digital photography. Kodak is a particularly important example as many of the technologies which make digital photography possible were owned by Kodak who, simply, did not take advantage of them. They were content to allow others to do that and failed to understand that customers wanted the image; the experience indeed the service, not the product. So the knowledge is not the critical factor governing the pace of change; it is the adaptability of institutions.

The leaders of organisations in 25 to 40 years' time are entering the jobs market and starting their careers now. Their views of the world are formed now by today's technologies and their ability to adapt their views declines rapidly. They become barriers to change; frequently interpreted as a negative quality but often a sane check on inappropriate changes. We should all be happy, or at least not unhappy, about this natural brake on the pace of change, as technology is there for our use.

Reinforcing this lethargy is the drag of invested capital. Invested capital is inherently conservative as it is slow to depreciate. Depreciation accounting and tax rules vary by country but for heavy capital assets such as steel mills they are seldom less than 15 years. Writing off the value of these assets sooner has a very negative impact on accounting results and, therefore, on career prospects for those who sanction this. Accounting and management practice also have a built-in mechanism to slow the process of technological renewal and replacement – marginal cash cost. Users of threatened technology will operate it at less than full cost in the attempt, usually successful, to delay its obsolescence and closure.

Steel replicates these characteristics. Electric arc furnaces were first used over 100 years ago. The basic oxygen furnace was invented around 1950 and not until the middle 1980's did the last open hearth furnaces close in North America. Some of the latter remain operational in ex-Soviet countries. Continuous casting was first introduced in the 1960s but did not mature in implementation until the 1990s. Indeed, it is still evolving. So for the period up to 2050, we can expect to be able to see today those technological changes which will affect the industry and its markets.

There is an apparent pattern of 35 years for major shifts in technology such as those just mentioned to move from first commercial application to generalised use. The reason is simple and relates directly to the length of executive careers, the rules of accounting depreciation and the other dynamics described above. There is nothing that can be foreseen that will change these fundamentals.

The focus of change

As always, the focus will be on lower costs involving: better yields, simplified processes, utilisation of lower cost raw materials and new product qualities. Great effort will go into new grades and coatings to produce new products to fit new and more demanding applications. These grade innovations however are not fundamental in the way that the EAF was. They do fascinate metals and engineering companies. There is truth in the observation that steel companies believe there is no problem of performance that cannot be solved by a new grade of steel. This is a flawed belief. The focus will be on the front and back end of the steel manufacturing process. There will be less to be gained by innovation in the central steel making and rolling operations. There is little economic incentive here as costs are already so low in basic steel making and rolling. Only being able to eliminate a stage in the process will there be significant impact on economic results and here there are innovations coming through which are considered below.

Lower cost raw materials

Here lies what many think of as a holy grail. For several decades some technologists and engineers have been foretelling the demise of the blast furnace. It is very capital intensive, has high fixed costs and has been around as the most prevalent way of making iron for centuries. It also works best with high grade and, thus, now high cost raw materials, and requires other processes and capital in the form of sinter or pellet plants and coke ovens; if only this could be simplified by removing some process stage or stages, substantial savings could follow in both operating and capital costs. Over the last two decades many innovations have been tried, mostly without any commercial success as yet. An example is HiSmelt which promises the ability to use both poorer quality coals without the coking requirement and high phosphorous iron ore for which there is no use at present. ITmK3 is another such process with similar objectives. Both these work but have failed to prove themselves commercially. POSCO's Finex process has commercial application but is not so fundamental an innovation.

Economics will eventually drive success in this area. Once the prize is big enough the challenges of one or more of these new technologies will be surmounted. There just needs to be a big enough prize at the end. The economic prize is what drives innovation. Until recently, this prize was not available. Throughout the 1980s and 90s the price of iron ore fell by over 1% p.a. in real terms and was only a quarter or less of its current price. The availability of high quality ore at low cost seemed assured. Then the growth of the Chinese industry happened and all raw material assumptions have been changed and for the long term. The economic target now is large, as was explained in an earlier chapter. There is approximately $400 in raw material in a tonne of steel - a tempting target.

The ultimate prize here is to be able to use titaniferrous-rich iron ores which normally come in the form of iron sands. These are very challenging to process economically due to the amount and nature of slag produced in the blast furnace. Iron sands with low iron content need beneficiation before charging to a BF which adds cost. But high Fe grade material still has the slag production issue. The increased slag requires extra energy to melt the gangue and to keep it liquid to avoid the tap holes becoming clogged. The normal way of accommodating to this problem is to redesign the BF with a wider hearth and lower height and raised tap holes. This solution is not perfect. If the company is able to process the slag downstream and recover the titanium and sometimes the vanadium then the economics can be attractive. A refined BF technology will be the answer to large scale use of these materials. An alternative such as rotary hearth furnaces will also emerge but the land footprint for rotary hearths precludes their use in many locations.

If breakthroughs could be achieved and matched by the use of non-coking coals; then the prize is very big indeed. The iron sands are surface material which can be scooped up and it is, normally, coastal so could be transported without rail or extensive road infrastructure. Moreover, there are hundreds of billions of tonnes of material. The economic prize can hardly be overemphasised. For example, if surface occurring iron sands could be used they would probably be at a cash cost of less than $20 /t against the marginal cash cost of current conventional ore at $100 or more. If this material could be processed using coal rather than coke then the savings per tonne of iron could easily exceed $200. Furthermore, if the Ti content could be extracted as a bi-product this could provide a very low cost feedstock for future titanium metal production like that being developed by companies such as Metalysis. We must assume the use of these materials will develop due to economic drivers which will incentivise the commitment of adequate research and development skill and money. However, the technical solution may be 10 years away and the full commercial availability probably 20 years away so this will come about within the timescale of this study but only perhaps towards the end; full proliferation of new processes will take longer. Current iron ore resources will have to suffice, at higher and higher cost, for a generation more.

Better yields

Opening up new raw material sources at low cost attacks the start or front end of the steel making process and is obviously attractive. The back end will also be a key focus. Yield loss in the making of steel has been a target for a long time. The increased integration of processes is attractive and this resulted in the development of continuous casting. This allowed for the elimination of the separate process of ingot casting with commensurate improvements in yield of all factors of production. Likewise, the evolution of continuous hot rolling mills has allowed for larger coils with reduced end and edge trimming and its resulting yield loss. Here, there is just emerging a process for casting very thin material which will eliminate the rolling of slabs to hot rolled strip; the most advanced and already commercial such process is Castrip, developed by BlueScope and Nucor. The prize here, essentially the ability to eliminate hot rolling and cold rolling for some applications, is big enough that a successful result is inevitable. These processes have been under development for 20 years so are just ready for commercial exploitation. The first patents for thin strip casting were taken out by Henry Bessemer in the middle of the 19th century as the desirability of the result was clear.

Yield loss in the use of steel in such processes as stamping and forging has been improving incrementally over a long period of time and made big strides forward in the last 30 years since the oil price shock mentioned earlier in the book. The ultimate goal is the use of powder to achieve a finished product or as close to that as is feasible. The goal is to achieve what is called near net shape processing; via casting or sintering. The more complex the part the more incentive there is to achieve this. A good example from outside steel is in the aerospace sector. Titanium is used for many parts such as in jet engines as it is light, but it is very expensive. A sheet of Ti metal will often cost $25,000 /t or more. A bar which could be used to form a turbine part will be the same. But these titanium parts are often complex in shape and lose 90% of their weight in the process of forming and machining and finishing the final part. The yield loss by value can be easily calculated. A prize of great magnitude is obtained if this part can be made from powder which can be formed to a near net final shape, perhaps requiring only final machining. The yield loss might be only 10%.

The same principle applies to many complex-shaped steel parts for car engines, domestic appliances, heavy equipment and capital goods of all types. One key limitation holding back the penetration of powder as a material has been the need for tools to take the female shape of the part to be formed. Now with the arrival of 3D printing and additive layer manufacturing, this limitation is no more. These new forming processes allow micron thick layers of material to be added onto each other via computer controlled lasers; the computer using a program with the actual 3 dimensional shape of the required part. The programs can be transmitted over the internet so as long as there is a supply of energy, of powder material of the right metallurgical properties and a machine to print: parts of any complexity can be made in batches of any size anywhere in the world.

As far as yield from a given amount of material is concerned, these developments are the end point. How far they could and will penetrate in steel use is unclear. I will assert that they will definitely take over for the production of complex parts for consumer and capital goods. Many of the suspension and drive train parts for example will benefit fundamentally from these changes; these are parts which are currently cast or forged and then machined. In total these many applications might amount to 25% of all steel use. When it comes to sheet, bar and section applications; these are much nearer to finished form already and these may remain rolled as solid rather than powder products.

Reductants

Iron ore contains oxygen which has to be removed to "reduce" the oxide ore to metal. The reductant is carbon and this is both expensive, being sourced from coking coal, and polluting. The resulting carbon dioxide is now regarded as a contributor to global warming, should that be occurring. It is possible to envisage other reductants such as electricity as in the electrolytic process for making aluminium, this could produce oxygen if it could be combined with an inert anode. Hydrogen is theoretically possible, which would potentially produce water as a bi-product which might become valuable in the future according to some forecasters who see the possibility of water shortages. However these reductants are not economically feasible today and it is difficult to see how they might become so as they require their independent prior production. These production costs and challenges will mitigate against their success.

Organising for innovation

Here is not the place to discuss the organisation of Research and Development resources, particularly people, for their effectiveness in achieving technological innovations. That is a large subject and was the subject of the first book I co-authored many years ago. What I will address here is how the steel companies should relate to these processes. Historically, steel companies had large R&D activities in house. These have been reduced greatly under the strains of poor financial performance. What remains is almost entirely devoted to the development of new products and grades. Process innovation, which is the subject of interest in this chapter, is now much more in the domain of independent technology and engineering companies such as Danieli, SMS, Siemens-VAI and the Japanese suppliers. This is obviously more efficient for the funding of development as these suppliers can amortise innovations over many customers whilst steel companies' in-house efforts are likely to be for their own use.

However, this benefit is also its limitation. Widely disseminated innovation is the "pyrrhic victory" described in the first section of the chapter. Only innovations unique to one or a few companies can result in long term financial benefit to those companies. Imagine what the discovery of the ability to process iron sands at low cost could do for the prospects of a steel company. This could be used to build highly competitive capacity in countries of growing steel use or to buy into established producers via trading the technology for shares in companies in more developed economies. It could be a mechanism for the inventing company to establish a dominant position in the industry.

The threat of substitution

Steel is by far the most common metal in use. The most important reason for this is its cheapness. When that is allied to its versatility of grade properties and, therefore, of its use -- its position is invincible.

Whilst, it is a mature product in age it is not mature as to its potential. There can be little doubt that there are many more usable grades to be discovered providing improved capabilities. There are ways of attacking the cost of basic iron making as discussed above. Steel is also already used in powder form and the innovations in powder processing will expand this application area immensely. Finally, there is the product's limitless capacity for recyclability.

Economics drives all in industry and this applies to a product's use and applications. It also applies to the innovative energy devoted to improvements in process and product. With the recent upward shift in the cost of conventional raw materials which will be permanent and the arrival of 3D Printing, we are at the start of a very exciting and innovative period for steel.

CHAPTER TWELVE

An industry for the 21st century

"Change is not made without inconvenience, even from worse to better." Samuel Johnson

Facilitating the future

My aim in this book has been to provide insights and ideas to assist the ferrous sector in general, and the steel industry in particular, to meet the challenges of today and benefit from the opportunities of tomorrow. I have played a part in the sector for the last 40 years and have devoted the greater portion of my professional time for the last 35 years to supporting its development. It is no idle fancy to say that I love the work that I do and the people I do it for and with – it is a truism of professional life that people like to do business with people they like. This has been true for me and I hope for those who have been kind and indulgent enough to employ me.

So what are my conclusions and how can I express them – as briefly as possible? I shall do this partly through descriptive summary and forecast, partly through explication of what I believe should be guiding principles of action to achieve the success I am convinced is available.

How much progress has been made....how much to come

The steel industry is not in as bad a condition as it has been in the past. The late 1970s and early 80s were a dire time, much worse than today in terms both of performance and of lack of understanding. I will use a scorecard approach to summarise and quantify how things have changed and will change.

Management gurus and consultants are fond of such devices as scorecards. They are always brief and come with a sometimes hidden methodology. They provide a simple if inevitably facile way of presenting complexity. They, also, often serve the provider's self-interest by being a means, through the use of the methodology, of selling a product and a process to clients. They should come with a health warning, but I am not trying to sell yet another management nostrum.

My scorecard makes no exotic claims to scientific value. It is based on no customer or producer survey. No questionnaires provide the basis for extensive statistical analysis to provide mind-numbing support for the observations. It is a summary of my practical, empirical experience of the last 40 years. It is based on project work for over 50 corporations and some governments and institutions in 40 countries and in every branch of the ferrous sector. For some of these companies, I have been involved in multiple assignments: the largest number was over 30. These assignments have often been carried out over many months and sometimes years; the longest individual assignment took three years. My professional exposure may not be unique but it is, I think, unusually broad and extensive. My experience provides a wide and heterogeneous sample, but it is only that. It includes a disproportionately small exposure to the Chinese industry and it is biased towards the English speaking world and the North Atlantic industry.

The industry of steel covers a great variety of types of companies, producing a vast array of products with a range of technologies, and occupying differing positions in the value chain. I can categorically state that no two companies I have worked for have been the same. My experience is also spread over a long period of time. Some may see that as a limitation. It vitiates against the scientific nature of my judgments. However, judgments are not scientific and my purpose in using this scorecard is to draw attention to how things have changed and how much yet remains to be changed. An elongated timescale and a complex set of examples are allies in that purpose. Because whatever the sample and whatever the experience has been, there have been very consistent patterns in what I have seen.

The focus and object of change is improved financial performance and my scorecard is designed to summarise my long examination of how the steel industry has improved its performance. My sample is limited to steel producers and I intend no reflection to be cast on raw material, technology or service suppliers. Indeed, these participants in the industry have systematically better performance than the core steel producers. The method is personal as well as judgmental; it is based on my judgment – no other friends or colleagues can be found wanting if the reader disagrees with me. Being based on extensive experience and a long fondness for the industry, I will claim that my views should, perhaps, be seen as an attempt at wisdom rather than science.

The scorecard

Exhibit 12.1 is the scorecard. I have taken a number of dimensions of performance which I believe to be strategic, that is where achievement is of long-term benefit and provides a major contribution to competitive advantage and financial success. All the dimensions are reflective of concerns and topics discussed at length in the body of the book; none should come as a surprise or need explanation as to why they are included. Well, no explanation to someone who has read the book – if you have skipped to the conclusion first, then you will need to go back and start at the beginning! Some topics may surprise by being excluded from the list, such as technology, product quality or consolidation.

The adoption of new technology in a timely and efficient manner is of great importance, but it is a supporting act to the whole drama of performance. Technology is a means to the end of either improved efficiency in the utilisation of the means of production or product quality and function. Product quality I regard as an element of customer service – one that is often over-emphasised but still very important. As will be clear from the early chapters, the product innovation of the industry has been and continues to be very good. However, there is a weakness in that such innovation is seen by some as an end in itself as a means to improved returns. This is a misunderstanding. Product innovation and improvement are only supports to improved customer service.

EXHIBIT 12.1: STEEL INDUSTRY SCORECARD (Max. 10)

Dimension	1983	2013	2028
Service and Customer	2	4	8
Managing Volatility	2	3	8
Managing Capacity	2	4	6
Efficiency in Use of Materials	3	7	8
Efficiency in Use of Energy	3	8	8
Efficiency in Use of Labour	2	6	8
Efficiency in Use of Capital	3	5	7
Degree of Appropriate Consolidation	2	4	6
Service to Shareholders	2	3	7
Total (out of 90)	21	44	66

Source: Author

Consolidation has been discussed at various points previously. It is a process with largely positive benefits, but again, gains made here will gradually be lost if improvement in service and the management of volatility are not achieved.

A general observation about the degree and speed of improvement is also a question. Being overly simplistic and numerical, I have suggested that the total level of improvement between 1983 and 2013 was 60%. I am also stating that the opportunity exists for a near 100% improvement between 2013 and 2028. This is a dramatic increase in the speed of change. My reasons are manifold. As I explained earlier, concerning general economic growth, systems learn how to grow, enabling faster growth; so Japan's early growth was faster than the USA's and China's faster than Japan's. The steel industry has also learnt. By improving, it has learnt that improvement is possible and within its own capability. For anyone not active in the industry in the late 1970s and early 80s, it is hard to perceive the degree of deep pessimism that existed in the steel industry at that time. The general view was that improvement was not within the power of the industry; nearly all depended on state intervention and even then maybe the future was one of permanent decline. The same tendency to blame external factors exists today, but with no such depth of negativity.

Some key developments are gravid with preparedness. The whole world of price risk management or insurance was new and full of fear only 10 years ago, as my own experience with the IISI (worldsteel) so amply demonstrated. Since then, iron ore spot pricing and related financial instruments have emerged strongly and are growing. In steel, the debate is alive and being won. At the Steel Success Strategies conference in New York in 2013, price risk hedging was the most discussed topic. Fear and anxiety still surround this issue but not as much as 10 years ago. In the area of service, the performance of the steel producers has improved enormously in certain key sectors such as automotive flat rolled. Outside Japan, the potential for improvements was unrecognised in 1973 and in its infancy in 1983. What has to happen now is to take that learning about service importance to all sectors of steel; the walls have been breached, the vanguard is established, now proliferation is required.

The industry today is in a healthier state than in 1983 and more able to progress. No significant North American steel producers have filed for Chapter 11 creditor protection, and no European companies have been nationalised during this extended recession. In addition, there are many new sources of energy and ideas today. The emergence of the Chinese, Indian, Middle Eastern and other industries provide new talent and perspectives. Organisations in all jurisdictions are more capable of self-generated change than they were 30 years ago. Change is no longer feared as it was so often and much managerial writing and teaching has concentrated on the processes to be used to manage change – although there will always be unpredictability and uncertainty. Over-arching all these improvements is the prevalence of information technology. The capacity of all social and economic systems to learn and develop today is enhanced more than we can calculate by the new information age.

Happy shareholders there will be

So, I do believe the level of improvement is required, as shown by current and historical financial performance, at the speed suggested. Most importantly, it is achievable. I have given many ideas as to how the dimensional improvements can be tackled and do not intend to repeat the story of previous chapters. Steel and ferrous generally stands at the start of a wonderfully exciting period of growth and enhanced performance. In the next decade or two, steelmaking will mature from an industry making the material required for a civilised life into an industry making the profits required to make happy shareholders. These prospects almost make me wish I was 30 or 40 years younger.

But, fundamental change there must be to achieve the achievable. Much of this change is in the approach to be taken to day-to-day management as well as long-term thinking. I have tried to show that the limits to growth are in our minds not in our means. Keynes was quoted at length in the prologue and I would reiterate how right he was then and is today, in the sentiments he expressed nearly 100 years ago in the depth of the depression. On a day-to-day level, I would encourage all industry participants to replace institutional inertia with venture vitality and to substitute energy for the natural forces of entropy which always exist in an industry as venerable as steel. We should not fear change; we should replace the fear with fun and the anxiety with anticipation.

A key is to align ourselves with Cassius, quoted at the start of the epilogue. In the same play, Brutus says: "There is a tide in the affairs of men, which, taken at the flood, leads on to fortune." Now is the tide for steel. There is still far too little faith that we can achieve the changes required and too much blame placed on outside circumstances.

This book has been written for those who side with Cassius and Brutus in the great questions of life: can we influence events or are they pre-determined; is the scope for our initiatives wide or narrowly constrained by circumstances?

The key to transformation is people

A central challenge the industry faces has been touched on and that is one of people. A hundred years ago, the steel industry was recognised as fundamental to economies. It was an exciting place to work, and metallurgy and engineering were frontier skills and disciplines. The period of steel's tribulations and financial underperformance has coincided with the emergence of the information technology sectors and many other new areas offering exciting prospects. Young people today have so many alternative career opportunities and many look more exciting and promising than to work for a steel company. This problem is most pronounced in North America, but it is global in scope.

In developing countries, it is still possible to work in steel and feel at the forefront of building the society and economy of which one is a part. Going to India always invigorates a belief in steel's future, but even here the Tata Sons group's most successful business over the last

10 years has been its systems business. Even here there is fierce competition for talent. So a key question for the industry is: how is it possible to attract good young talent to an industry so pessimistic about itself and which readily admits to not knowing how to return itself to financial viability? Most importantly, who would work for a company which might not survive to provide a full career and pay a pension? The biggest underlying challenge for steel is the talent shortage.

The answer to the above rhetorical questions is – no one! The industry needs to transform its beliefs about itself before it can attract the talent required to achieve the transformation in its performance. The leaders need to be positive and to exude that positivism; whatever the challenges, leaders must believe they can be met and overcome.

Yet the story I have laid out here is exciting – what is more so? I started this exercise thinking to write the book I would have liked to have had available to read in 1974, when I started working in this sector. Then, as now, pessimism was rampant – but it was then, as now, not appropriate. The industry needs to grasp the meaning it has for the world economy and to "sell the story". Of course, first it will have to understand what the exciting story is; I hope to have demonstrated that. Then the leaders of the industry have to believe in it. I suggest that there needs to be a wide debate about the future and a much deeper understanding of the strategic situation, a debate that I do not think is being conducted today. I hope to have made a contribution here. There is a great opportunity and it is for young, talented people to fulfil that opportunity and achieve great things - but they must be told and enthused!

The danger of simplistic forecasts

I have sought throughout this book to avoid forecasting of the spuriously definite sort. I have taken the approach that stargazing into the future is best seen as a form of reflection on the past, used to envision the likely shape of future outcomes. Forecasting tells us a lot about the forecaster but seldom a lot about the future. Today this is too often forgotten as we are besotted by the power of computer models. We forget the oldest of all computer science directives – GIGO: Garbage In Garbage Out. It is the assumptions and the envisioning logic that are important, not the model, which is at best derived from those starting points. Often these origins are not even acknowledged, so no critical assessment can be made of them.

What is needed has little to do with forecasting and a lot to do with creative interpretation. As I hope I have demonstrated on a number of occasions: what the industry has believed on the basis of credible forecasts has often turned out to be fallacious.

Human aspirations can and will be met

On this basis, I believe the human search for a better life will proliferate across the planet. Modern communications make this inevitable as a desire. Its achievement might be stopped, and then only might be, by some catastrophe. Every century has its difficulties. Underlying the growth of the world is simple human aspiration; the industry needs not just to exploit and meet this but take advantage of what it means in individual human terms. The drama plays out through individuals in organisations; through talent used in pursuit of social and organisational goals. The industry needs to gain its share of those human energies. Human aspiration implies the growth of market opportunity but it also implies the opportunity for talent recruitment. Individuals want to achieve successful and exciting outcomes in their productive lives; steel presents great opportunities for such successes.

Geographical distribution of opportunity

The world of steel will look different in 50 years' time, but this will not just be globally. It will also look very different by geography. This relates directly to the need to attract talent. Some zones with the greatest opportunities have the greatest intensity of competition for human talent. There are some "old" steel zones which will surprise; we have dealt with China in an earlier chapter.

North America

North America will show much stronger growth than anyone imagines – or at least anyone I speak to. I have suggested earlier that this century will be an American century. Steel there will have strong growth. There are many reasons for this: population growth will be consistent and steady; economic growth will be sustained and may accelerate, at least for the next two decades; shale gas is real and supports a general rise in the growth rate; "on-shoring" will become strong for the next decade or perhaps longer. Underpinning everything is the fundamental attractiveness of manufacturing in America: flexible labour markets; an entrepreneurial culture; developed capital markets; efficient transport; a large open market; raw materials in volume, etc. As we have seen, the economy is much more steel-intensive than is generally understood. This offers a very large opportunity for steel growth. Not all this steel will be on-shored but some should and will be.

Finally, America has two steel industries. The old BF-based industry has declined and is now less than 40% of capacity. Decline will continue. There is the EAF industry whose modern form was born in the USA and has flourished there. This sector will grow strongly and provides the model for the future, and the skills and organisational models and learning required. Comparative advantage in steel making is shifting towards North America: EAF production favours local production as scrap is a local raw material. The largely raw material poor countries in my top 20 are unlikely to become net steel exporters. This is also true of India where production will likely lag behind demand growth. I am happy to hazard a forecast that by 2050 North American steel production will be two to three times as big as today.

Europe and the 20

European steel is in a distressed state today. This is not helped by the general sclerotic malaise of Europe's economy under the continuing Euro crisis, and over-regulation from Brussels which focuses on social solidarity and harmonisation rather than innovation and individual entrepreneurialism. All of this is overhung by wildly optimistic, and unachievable, ambitions in carbon reduction. A period of success in the first decade of the century has been replaced by circumstances reminiscent of the 1980s. Europe's abilities to meet its economic challenges are being sacrificed on the altar of political objectives - "an ever closer union" as enshrined in the Treaty of Rome. The Euro project is just the latest manifestation of this priority. Yet the history of the last 200 years has been one of economics triumphing over politics. So this folly will end. The economic interests of the Europeans will triumph. One does not know how, but this will occur. The strengths of Europe, which lie in its complexity and hence creativity, will be released again and they will play a part in the revitalisation of the steel sector.

Those strengths are technological in both product and process and also include an acceptance of outside investment. Perhaps 50% of European steel capacity is now owned by non-European companies. These new Europeans, Indians, Brazilians, Russians in particular, are well placed to facilitate much of the growth in the top 20 and beyond which I highlighted earlier. This would benefit from the help of Europe as the most international of industries and with deep technological and operating skills. In the shorter term the emerging markets will represent a major export opportunity.

Don't panic

The 20th century had its fair share of doomsters predicting the destruction of the planet by the actions of mankind. This has been a theme of this book. What links all these doom-laden forecasts is the reading of too much into first consequences and not enough into the unforeseen ones. Indeed, the end of the world will happen and the human race will be extinguished just as happened with the dinosaurs. Darwin will be proved correct, all species have their niche and when that disappears so does the species; although the accuracy of his theories will not bring very much benefit to the human race. In the meantime, the human race must use what tools are available to it to meet its challenges. Man has discovered that by the application of human intelligence the world can be comprehended and that comprehension can be converted into enhanced capability through technology. This is the ultimate miracle. To borrow from Einstein: "The eternal mystery of the world is its comprehensibility...The fact that it is comprehensible is a miracle." Whilst admiring the man, I do not go along with him on thinking about the future: "I never think about the future. It comes soon enough." Perhaps he was making an observation about the ultimate luxury of being an intellectual in the comfortable arms of Princeton University.

Innovation will not displace steel

Steel is the fundamental material needed for the great development of the 21st century which will see the poor 75% of the planet become wealthy, or we are all likely to perish in the failure. In terms of materials, the 21st century will be a century of steel. There is no material which is remotely conceivable today which will challenge the pre-eminence of this material. Technical change will occur. Improvements in steel's qualities will continue and so will its efficiency in production. The blast furnace will be finally replaced by EAFs and by new iron-making processes which allow for the efficient use of poor quality ores and cheaper coals or other reductants.

In competitive materials, gains will be made only on the fringes of total metal needs. Titanium, for instance, will emerge as a much lower-cost product than today and with very desirable properties: not difficult as it is $25,000 /t of sheet or even more. But even if it were to grow in use by 10% p.a. for 50 years, it would only be an industry of 10Mt. Likewise with aluminium, a metal which has already been in use for over 100 years: growth of 5% p.a. would result in a demand of 150Mt by 2050. This is to be compared with my expectation of demand for steel being close to 4bnt p.a. by 2050 and 6bnt by 2100. I do not believe in the early arrival of "Peak Steel". The key to steel's continuing pre-eminence is that it has an unusual affinity with other elements which allow for an ever-expanding range of alloys and, therefore, applications and it has this at very low comparable cost. I cannot see this advantage being displaced.

Now, I readily admit that by my own logic of innovation and the inherent limitations of forecasting, I may be surprised, or, rather, I would be surprised if I was not surprised. Assuming, that is, that I am around later in the century. In the words of Donald Rumsfeld, "there are known unknowns and unknown unknowns", and it is the latter that can surprise for sure. There are materials such as graphene which might surprise, and manufacturing technologies such as additive layer manufacturing which might fundamentally change the use of materials. But these two are known unknowns; of more concern is what we cannot even envisage today. During the 20th century, new technologies emerged which even the science-fiction writers of the time did not foresee. We must expect such unexpected events with ever-increasing frequency during this century. What an exciting time it will be for our grandchildren.

Additive layer manufacturing and 3D printing represent potentially large breakthroughs as they take the theme of yield improvement to another level. Much of the economic improvement in metals - their lower costs - is due to yield improvements. The use of powder, required for these new processes, is a next stage in this history. This does not disadvantage steel as already iron and steel metal powders exist and are used in sintering processes. The technologies will assist titanium to grow as it is very expensive in solid form and suffers more yield loss in component manufacturing than any other metal. Hence it has the most to gain.

Financial woes can be overcome

The major hypothesis of this monograph is that the industry stands poised on the brink of a major transformation which it can itself facilitate - hence, the book's sub-title. This is a once-in-a-generation, or even once-in-a-lifetime, opportunity. It is one that could, if seized and exploited, set the industry on a century-long path of financial success. We have been obsessed for a decade with the importance of the BRIC countries for the economic growth of the world. Indeed, they are important, but they are by no means everything. For steel this is especially true. China is maturing in steel use: there will be further growth but it will now be much slower. India will be important, but Russia is irrelevant; it is a country of declining population which already produces a volume commensurate with the living standards of the USA. Brazil is a country of less than 200M with an ever disappointing achievement record and unfulfilled promise.

The next largest countries are full of promise and opportunity; they are what I have called the top 20. How these will provide their steel requirements is one transformational opportunity. Here there are already over 1.7bn people and there will be over 2.6bn by 2050 - twice China's current population. Steel consumption is already twice that of India and production less than consumption by 20Mt. Raw materials are limited and scarce in most of these countries, in this they differ fundamentally from the BRICs, but growth rates in 12 already exceed 5% p.a. By 2050 their steel demand will exceed that of China today. It will not be economically efficient or rational for most of them to be self-sufficient. Should the established steelmakers be able to deploy the capital then they could take a lead in fulfilling this demand, in consort with local entrepreneurs, and avoid the need for state funding. This would avoid the curse of uncoordinated capacity expansion and unfair competition. After the 20, there is also the rest of the world's population to consider: a further mere 1.5bn. The established producers need to see this opportunity, to understand that they have the skill sets and capabilities to assist here to their own advantage as well as that of the countries concerned.

...and will be

If the needs of the next generation of growing countries can be met with the active participation of current producers, then the financial future for them will look bright. However, to fulfil this destiny requires better financial performance today and tomorrow: in fact immediately. The change is urgently required. The current challenges must be met and overcome. I have examined how to do this in depth in previous chapters but the key change which needs to be grasped is to reverse the management culture of giving priority to capacity utilisation and production volume. This needs to be replaced by a priority on service. Providing close to 100% service to all customers is needed.

This will align steel with the priority driver of other industries, including those described today as manufacturing. It will replicate steel's own approach to supplying the automotive sector. Furthermore, and of the greatest importance, it will improve the economics of their customers and enable steel to charge higher prices and achieve higher margins. This will improve the returns on capital. As they work the culture of service, with its concomitants of just-in-time and lean manufacturing, through the steelmaking process, they will optimise operations in a new and more efficient way so achieving further margin gains. These gains will suffer less pressure in the inevitable downturns as the service level will breed a much higher level of mutual commitment. Customers will have a much lower incentive to switch suppliers in search of marginally lower prices. A new and virtuous circle will develop between supply and demand.

The second great change required is to embrace the inevitability of cyclicality and to craft a virtue out of a vice. The way to handle volatility and mitigate the consequences of its risks, learning here from a multitude of other risks accommodated by human beings, is to utilise price risk management tools. The reluctance to do so and the claimed reasons for the reluctance have been examined in some depth. Not only would the embracing of these tools be beneficial for financial performance and, hence, lower the cost of capital for the industry; they would also offer a further enhancement to the marketing of steel products. Price risk is a larger challenge to customers than it is to producers. Steel companies should offer PHM tools as a service to their customers. They are in a great position to do this, being large sophisticated organisations with the capacity to construct packages of service at low cost, sharing the fixed cost of this across a multitude of customers. This would be a service on which they could make a supplementary profit and it would tie customers even more strongly to suppliers, enhancing brand loyalty. The first steel groups to do this and to break ranks from the industry consensus will gain a very significant competitive advantage. Here a vice can be converted into a virtue: a piece of 21st century alchemy.

The provision of service could progress even further. As steel companies become more profitable as they embrace these transformational opportunities, they could become underwriters of their customers' working capital. Although much attention is focused on major customers - after all they can create the most negative publicity and noise and their orders carry the most clout - the steel market is made up of tens of millions of small customers. These are the small and medium-sized businesses which form the backbone of any economy: wire drawers, tubers, roll formers, forgers, structural fabricators etc. In general, these have weak balance sheets, little leverage over their banks and find working-capital provision a challenge. This is especially so in downturns. These circumstances are little different from the automotive sector. The answer in that sector is semi-independent finance houses, providing finance to car buyers, facilitating purchases and constituting a new profit source. This is not dissimilar to how GE developed their finance arm.

The sum total of the changes I propose and the initiatives I advocate will be to make the industry financially successful and self-sustaining, thus not requiring the provision of state capital. Achieving the service levels which are possible will enhance margins by several percentage points. The embracing of PRM for the producers will reduce the cost of capital by at least a percentage point and probably 2, whilst the provision of such tools to customers will provide an excellent further enhancement of margins. Should the financing of working capital for customers be feasible this will provide a further return. The objective of enhancing EBITDA returns by 7 - 8% across the cycle is eminently achievable.

Be confident ...act now

I am confident in the future of steel. Its prospects are brighter now than since 1946. The capacity for the human being to learn and adapt is infinite and, despite the current gloom and despondency, for those who do adapt and learn new ways of managing the business and serving its customers, success awaits. How the transformation I propose will start, I don't know. Some individual companies are beginning to experiment with the new tools available and the new strategies that can be pursued; if they prove successful then others will follow. This is the most likely evolution. The sector's communal institutions could play a part. The most important of these is the World Steel Association. This does a great deal of good work but I think focuses on the wrong issues. It is very good at sharing better practices across companies, developing approaches to technical challenges such as light-weighting of vehicles and other such communally benevolent issues. These do not strike at the core of the industry's malaise. Where is the promotion of financial performance improvement, improved service levels and other changes which would enhance prospects at a deeper level?

Further, what help is being provided to those countries beyond the BRICs? It is not just a time for a new development agenda for individual companies but for the industry as a whole.

EPILOGUE

"Men are at some time masters of their fate. The fault, dear Brutus, is not in our stars but in ourselves" Julius Caesar, Act 1, Scene 2.

Now I am at the end of this journey, the adventure of writing. It is time to attempt a summary. Writing this book has been a process of learning. I believe my ideas have been matured and deepened by the process which has been a source of enjoyment. Indeed the writing has been great fun; although a much larger task than I expected at the start. I have found the reading, re-reading, adjusting, adding, subtracting, editing and responding to others' ideas and suggestions – not always to their satisfaction – has taught me more than I expected and shown me more of my thinking than I was aware of at the beginning.

I believe even more strongly than I did in the wisdom of the two statements in my prologue. The two central observations in those quotations remain absolutely true and reinforced in my thinking. Paraphrasing these statements; the CEO of the world's 6th largest steel company called for the industry to re-invent itself, whilst Keynes, perhaps the most influential economist of the 20th century, stated that the world was solving its economic problems and people would be 4 to 8 times better off in 100 years than when he was writing in 1930. He believed in the achievement of human aspirations in the face of overwhelming pessimism.

The steel industry has to change; more than it has in the past and more than it generally acknowledges now. Areas of great self-awareness exist. These are isolated areas and not broad and deep enough yet to bring about the changes which are needed. The future of the world and its economic development can be is envisaged and represents a great opportunity for steel and its companies and people. Without change these opportunities will be lost: or rather fulfilled but in a state driven and disappointing, distressing fashion. Growth is inevitable; steel is a true foundation industry, it underpins and supports all other economic development and this will not change in this century; if the private sector will not meet this need then the state will.

The future viability and the health of any social or economic institution lies in the people it can attract and enthuse to work on its behalf. Steel is failing here. No industry can attract the talent it requires if it is not positive and enthusiastic about its future. Not only that; it must believe in its own ability to solve its problems and meet its challenges. Who can expect to attract the quantity and quality of talent it desires and needs if these attitudes are not present? Who can expect others to believe what they do not believe themselves?

The talent is required to deliver a new vision of steel: one driven by the ideas of the 21st century not the 19th. The industry must look to the future and not the past. It needs to focus on what it needs to do now, not on what it has done; even though that is great and worthy of acclaim and admiration. Central to all this is achieving a much higher level of profitability which will feed the high levels of capital required to deliver the growth required. If it does not do this then the state will provide – but the consequences will be as negative as they have been in the past when the state has provided.

Self-sufficiency in capital is achievable. The keys to this lie in themes which will dominate wealth creation over the coming decades. Service is what consumers need and want. They will obtain it. The volatility in financial markets and economic cycles will continue and may even become more extreme as the world's economic system integrates and expands over the century. Price risk insurance - in buying and selling - is the mechanism to make the volatility more manageable and less damaging.

Human aspirations exist in the developing world for better living conditions, to match those current in the developed world. These aspirations cannot be denied and they will be met; somehow or other. Capitalism provides the best, most efficient and effective and, most importantly, most humane way to meet these needs. A key to all economic growth has been and remains globalisation. This phenomenon is not new, it underlies all growth and it is only the process of economic specialisation and comparative advantage, which started in Mesopotamian villages, at the level of the globe. So globalisation will continue; it implies and requires increasing levels of economic and organisational interdependence. Steel can and must respond to this implication. Globalisation requires higher levels of profitability and will reinforce these levels, creating a virtuous circle.

I hope you have enjoyed the reading as much as I have enjoyed the writing. If you are involved in the steel sector then enjoy the ride over the coming decades; it will be turbulent, rewarding and fun.

GLOSSARY

BF	Blast furnace
BOF	Basic oxygen furnace
BRIC	Brazil, Russia, India and China
CFR	Cost and freight
CRU	Commodities Research Unit
DRI	Direct reduced iron
EAF	Electric arc furnace
EBIT	Earnings before interest and tax
EBITDA	Earnings before interest, tax, depreciation and amortisation
FOB	Free on board
FCF	Fixed capital formation
GDP	Gross domestic product
IRR	Internal rate of return
LME	London Metal Exchange
OCTG	Oil country tubular goods
PCI	Pulverised coal injection
PRHM	Price risk hedging mechanisms
ROC	Return on capital
TSU	Total steel use
TSI	The Steel Index
WACC	Weighted average cost of capital
WSA	World Steel Association or worldsteel (Previously IISI – International Iron and Steel Institute)

bn	billion
k	1000kg
Mt	million tonnes
tonnes	standard metric measure in international markets. 1,000 kilogrammes
t p.a.	tonnes per annum
trn	trillion

ABOUT THE AUTHOR

Rod Beddows received his first degree in Philosophy and Politics from Bristol University in the UK. After a period in the Information Technology sector he attended Business School and obtained an MSc from Durham and a doctorate from Harvard University School of Business. He held academic positions and served as a Visiting Senior Research Fellow at Harvard. Whilst he was there he co-authored a book entitled; "Managing Large Scale Research and Development Programs".

From 1979 he owned and ran his own Strategy Consulting firm gradually focusing on the Ferrous sector. Later he sold the business to Hatch Associates, a major technology and engineering firm specializing in the Mining and Metals sectors and joined their board. Recently he has co-founded a boutique financial advisory firm focused on the same sectors. His clients are confidential but have comprised most of the major firms and many minor ones in the ferrous value chain.

Email: rbeddows@hcfintl.com

Printed in Great Britain
by Amazon